erika knight

simple knits for cherished babies

photography by john heseltine

COLLINS & BROWN

First published in the United Kingdom in 2003
This edition first published in 2008 by
Collins & Brown
10 Southcombe Street
London
W14 0RA

An imprint of Anova Books Company Ltd

Distributed in the United States and Canada by
Sterling Publishing Co, 387 Park Avenue South, New York,
NY 10016-8810, USA

ISBN 978-1-84340-478-1

A CIP catalogue for this book is available from the British Library.

10 9 8 7 6 5 4 3 2 1

Reproduction by Rival Colour Ltd, UK
Printed and bound by SNP Leefung, China

Keep updated. Email crafts@anovabooks.com

This book can be ordered direct from the publisher.
Contact the marketing department, but try your bookshop first.

www.anovabooks.com

simp 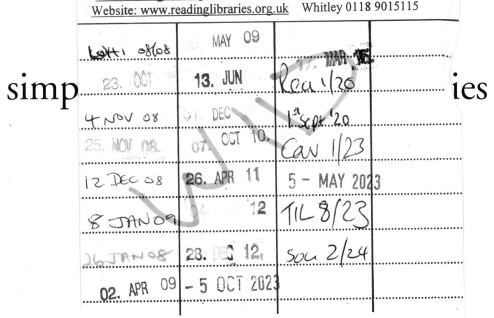 ies

Author:
Title:

Class no.

**To avoid overdue charges please return this book to a
Reading library on or before the last date stamped above.
If not required by another reader, it may be renewed by
personal visit, telephone, post, email, or via our website.**

It has been a great opportunity with the creation of this new edition, to revisit the values and the yarns that lay behind the designs and original intention of this book. Babies grow and new babies arrive, but the ethos is the same. Yarns and colours are subject to the vagaries of time, but are often replaced by newer, more beautiful fibres. This has proved a timely opportunity to revise and add to the repertoire of materials to make these simple knits that little bit special!

Knitting for a new baby is always a great pleasure • The baby has a wonderful quality of newness, freshness and purity, and the whole joy and excitement of a new life creates a great rush of enthusiasm and creativity, as well as a desire to personalize the event • This desire to cherish, protect and nurture any young creature is very strong • How nice, then, if you can find some tangible way in which to express these feelings • Time is precious, so if someone knits for you, or you for them, the gift is very special • If a friend or relative is expecting a baby, it is a real pleasure to create something yourself, as an act of love, and then present it as a special gift for the new arrival – the smallness of the garments brings out the maternal instinct in all of us • Classically designed baby garments look as good in twenty years' time, creating heirloom pieces for a future generation of children.

This book contains a selection of traditional baby garments, with a slightly modern twist • The colour palette is soft, muted tones of chalky pastels, representing a return to more traditional colour values, and a move away from the primary colour brights of the last few years • There are three weights of yarn used: chunky, for hardwearing cardigans and blankets; medium for updated classic garments, and fine for garments chosen for their softness next to the skin: a tiny vest, for example, or a little pair of silk slippers for a new-born baby's delicate feet.

The design ideas in this book are informed by a few basic, but simple, rules • With tops for babies, any openings must go easily over the baby's head and the garments must slip on and off as easily as possible • The pattern instructions are written in simple language, without confusing abbreviations • The patterns generally contain few special techniques, and where these are required, a cross reference is made to an explanation at the back of the book • The only other referrals in the patterns are to charts, which are also given for the relevant projects in a special section at the back of the book.

The stitches used in the projects contained in this book are simple: primarily stocking (stockinette) stitch, garter stitch and simple knit and purl rib, with a few special touches included to give these essentially plain garments a singularly beautiful finish. Casting on on a size smaller needle to produce a firmer edge, a few simple increasing and decreasing ideas to create a fully fashioned sleeve setting, a little picot trim or an integral button band, for example, can make a surprising difference to the finished look of the garment.

The yarns chosen for these patterns are all natural ones – cottons, silks and fine wools. They are soft and gentle on young skins, and they have the virtue of washing and wearing extremely well. Small enough to fit into a bag, the projects lend themselves to being knitted at odd moments – on planes, trains and buses, or in the lunch hour at work, or even while waiting in the wings of a hospital. It is important, particularly when knitting with delicate yarns in pale colours, to keep the work clean. While you knit, keep your needles, yarn and a copy of the pattern together in a simple bag (like the little organza one shown opposite) to protect your work. It will do duty later as a gift bag.

Knitted gifts should be presented beautifully, as befits the trouble you have taken in making them, so take the time to pack up the garments or other projects attractively. Ideas are given on pages 106–7.

erika knight

getting started

about **yarns and needles**

EACH BABY is special and unique, and the garments we make for them should echo these qualities and offer softness, warmth and protection. Time spent selecting delicate soft natural yarns suitable for babies will never be wasted, nor will the money spent on the best quality ones. Cashmere, silk, fine merino wool, and cotton, are a little more expensive to purchase than more traditionally available yarns designed for babies, but each have a very special quality. They provide luxurious softness to cocoon and cosset, and to keep babies warm in winter and cool in summer. Natural fibres allow the body to breathe, absorb moisture and circulate the air around a baby's delicate body, and they wash and wear with a quality second to none. **Cashmere** is a noble fibre and the ultimate in luxury. It is ultra soft, light and beautiful to the touch. **Silk** has a renowned natural sheen and also an exquisite drape.

It is luxurious and sensuous to the touch. **Fine merino wool** is strong and flexible, making it a joy to knit with as it creates a smooth, elegant fabric that keeps its shape well. It is warm in winter, cool in summer and does not crease. **Botany wool** is strong and light, but also warm. **Cotton** has a natural look and is soft and cool to the touch. It is available matt or shiny, smooth, slubby or textured. It is hardwearing and easy to wash. You need very little yarn to create garments for small babies. The tiny projects for new babies take just a ball or two of wool or silk. Depending on the size or weight of the yarn, you will need the appropriate needles. Bamboo needles are particularly suited to fine work, being wonderfully smooth. You will need relatively few sizes for the patterns in this book, the sizes needed being given at the start of each pattern.

about **tension (gauge)**

opposite: Graded from left to right, three principal weights of yarn – fine, medium and chunky – in cotton, silk and wool are shown with suitably sized bamboo needles alongside. The pattern instructions in the book explain which yarn weights and needle sizes are needed for each project.

IF YOU WANT THE PROJECTS you knit to be the correct size, your knitting must be the correct tightness or tension. Tension is the term given to the number of stitches and rows you should have to the centimetre/inch you knit on the given needles, yarn and stitch pattern. For accurate sizing, the tension must be correct. If you knit too tightly, your garment will be too small; if you knit too loosely, your garment will be too large. Every project instruction will give you the yarn, needles and tension required for that particular project. To check your tension, knit a sample square slightly larger than 10cm (4in) using the yarn, needles and stitch requested. Smooth the square out on a flat surface without stretching it. Then, using a ruler, mark out a 10cm (4in) square in the knitting and count every stitch and half stitch; check this number against the tension requested. Count the rows in the same way. If you have too many stitches and rows your knitting is too tight, and you will need to use a size fatter needle. If you have too few stitches and rows it is too loose, and you will need to knit with a size finer needle.

above: The same yarn is knitted on three different sizes of needle to illustrate how tension will affect the finished size of your project. The tension in the centre is the correct size. On the left the tension is too tight and on the right it is too loose. To adjust the tension, a change in needle size is needed.

about the **patterns**

opposite: Three little vests
demonstrate the variation in
sizes depicted in the project
instructions: 0–3 months, 3–6
months and 6–9 months
respectively.

THE PATTERNS IN THIS BOOK are written following normal pattern writing conventions. The instructions are written out in full, whenever possible, with as much information as it is feasible to give to make them easy to follow. Where there is a repeating instruction within the pattern, this passage is marked with asterisks. Where special techniques, such as increasing and decreasing or making an eyelet, are needed, this is indicated at the beginning of the pattern and a cross-reference given to the explanation, which is listed at the back of the book on page 124. The technique is then incorporated into the pattern following the normal pattern writing convention.

sizing

Even new born babies vary greatly in size, from a premature baby weighing just a few pounds to an extra large baby whose birth weight is equal to that of a naturally small, three-month-old baby. It is important, therefore, not to go merely by age, but to work out actual sizes. If you are knitting in advance for a baby, guess at one of the middle sizes or, if the parents' family history indicates large babies, go for the biggest size – the baby will grow into it! Instructions are given in three sizes for each project, worked out on averages of age and weight but are intended as a guide only. In each pattern, the first instructions are given for the smallest size and the figures inside the brackets refer to the next sizes up. The sizing has been worked out to allow a little extra room for comfort. The three little vests shown here show the different sizes included in the instructions, 0–3 months, 3–6 months, 6–9 months. At the back of the book on pages 112–115 are details of the projects, with the actual baby measurements for which each size is intended, as well as the finished sizes of the knitted garments. To ensure the garments are the correct size, you should measure the baby first, if you can.

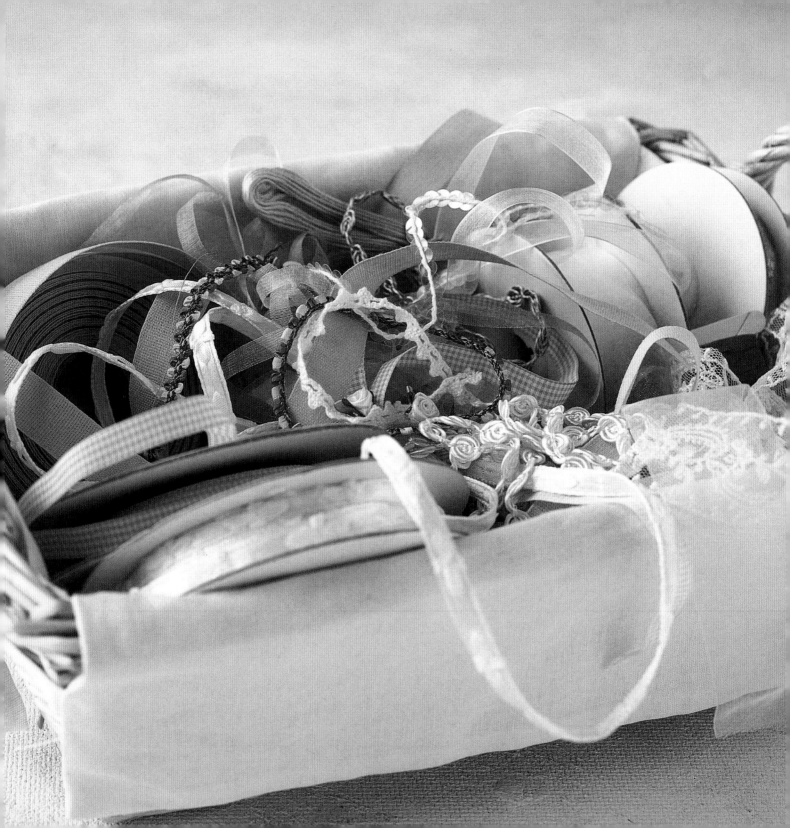

about **trims & embellishments**

left: Look for attractive trimmings, collecting and hoarding remnants saved from favourite discarded clothes or scour charity shops and jumble sales for pretty and individual embellishments and buttons.

above: These simple little slippers have been given a delightful finishing touch by applying fine braid around the ankles.

JUST AS MUCH ATTENTION should be paid to the choice of trimmings as to the selection of yarn, as only too often a beautifully crafted garment is spoiled by inferior or cheap buttons or synthetic ribbon trims. It does take time to source interesting and beautiful trims and embellishments, but if you find it difficult to do through conventional stores you may choose to recycle from favourite discarded clothes or you can scour charity shops for more unique and unusual items to personalize your projects. Most of the projects shown in this book are enhanced by the addition of the right trim in matching colours and suitable fabrics. Some of the simplest are the most delightful: organza ribbons in pale colours, washed-cotton tapes, fine decorative braids, tiny mother of pearl buttons, satin roses, cross-stitch embroidery, fine silk ribbons and antique lace. Take care when applying any trims or embellishments to do so as neatly as possible using appropriate matching thread and small, neat stitches.

warning

None of the garments or their trims must be dangerous for the baby in any way. Buttons must be securely fixed with button thread so that they cannot be pulled off and swallowed. Ribbons must be fixed in such a way that babies cannot choke on them or strangle themselves with them.

knitting for the baby

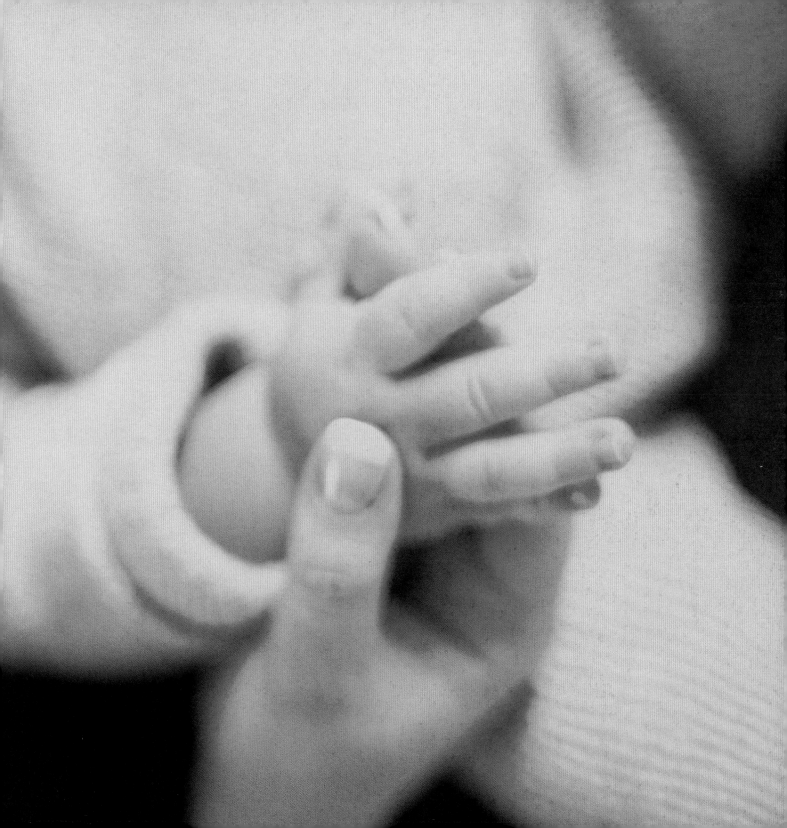

classic cashmere sweater

Cashmere is the ultimate yarn for comfort and luxury – nothing but the best for the new addition to the family! However, this simple stocking (stockinette) stitch sweater can also be knitted in merino wool or cotton, if you prefer. It is made in one piece, and is very easy to knit. The garter stitch hems add a modern finishing touch, as do the washed-cotton tape ties at the neck opening. The slit in the centre back makes it really easy to slide the sweater over the baby's head. The sweater can be combined with the leggings (see page 26) and the bootees (see page 32) to create a matching outfit for your baby.

how to make: **classic cashmere sweater**

SIZING: For sizing refer to chart on page 112.

MATERIALS: 3 (3:4) x 25g balls 4 ply yarn eg. Jaeger cashmere (which knits as a medium yarn) • Pair of 3.75mm (US 5) needles • Sewing needle • Cotton tape approximately 46cm (18in) in length • Sewing cotton to match tape

TENSION (GAUGE): 22 stitches and 32 rows to 10cm (4in) square measured over stocking (stockinette) stitch using 3.75mm (US 5) needles.

above: This is simple and easy to knit, worked in one piece. The slit at the back is made by dividing the stitches and working on each set of stitches in turn.

opposite: The soft natural luxury of cashmere, delicate "fashioned" detailing at the neck edge, the little garter stitch welt and the turned back cuffs (for growing room) are all classic features.

TECHNIQUES: Slip the first stitch and knit the last stitch of every row on the sleeves; this will give a neat appearance when the sleeves are turned back. Cast on and cast off evenly, not too tightly, as this will ensure a neat edge. The only other technique required is knitting through the back of the loops (see page 124).

METHOD: Using 3.75mm (US 5) needles, cast on 52 (60:68) stitches. Work 6 rows in garter stitch; every row knit. Now change to stocking (stockinette) stitch and continue until work measures 12.5 (15:18)cm/5 (6:7)in.

right: The neck opening is made by casting off the centre stitches and working on each set of stitches in turn. The shaping is worked two stitches in from the edge to give a soft, neat appearance.

below: To give a neat finish to the centre slit, the first stitch of every row is slipped onto the right needle.

opposite: When the garment is sewn up, the side seams are left unstitched at the garter stitch band to give a little side vent detail.

SHAPE SLEEVES: Cast on 34 (40:46) stitches at the beginning of the next 2 rows. *(120 (140:160) stitches)* Continue on these stitches until the knitting measures 18.5 (22:25.5)cm/7 (8$^{1}/_{2}$:10)in, ending with a purl row.

SHAPE NECK: Knit 53 (63:72) stitches, cast off the centre 14 (14:16) stitches, knit to the end of the row. Now work on each set of stitches in turn.
Row 1: slip the first stitch, purl to end (neck edge).
Row 2: knit 2 stitches, knit the next 2 stitches together through the back loops, knit to the end of the row. Work these last 2 rows twice more. Work straight until knitting measures 21.5 (25:29)cm/8$^{1}/_{2}$ (10:11$^{1}/_{2}$)in, ending with a purl row.

TO MAKE THE CENTRE BACK SPLIT: Cast on 11 (11:12) stitches at the beginning of the next row. Now work on these 61 (71:81) stitches for a further 7 (8:9)cm/2³/₄ (3¹/₄: 3³/₄)in, ending with a purl row. Break yarn and leave the stitches on the needle or a length of yarn.

NOW WORK THE OTHER SIDE: With the wrong side of the work facing, rejoin yarn to neck edge and purl to the last stitch, knit it. **Row 1:** knit to the last 4 stitches, knit 2 stitches together, knit 2 stitches. **Row 2:** purl to the last stitch, knit it. Work these last 2 rows twice more. Work straight until the knitting measures 21.5 (25:29)cm/8¹/₂ (10:11¹/₂)in, ending with a knit row.
Cast on 11 (11: 12) stitches at the beginning of the next row. Now work on these 61 (71:81) stitches for a further 7 (8:9)cm, 2³/₄ (3¹/₄:3³/₄)in, ending with a purl row.

Next row: knit across all the stitches from both halves, knitting the 2 centre stitches together. *(121 (141:161) stitches)* Work straight until knitting measures 9 (10:11.5)cm/3¹/₂ (4: 4¹/₂)in from back neck edge. Cast off 34 (40:46) stitches at the beginning of the next 2 rows. *(53 (61:69) stitches)* Continue to knit for a further 10.5 (13:16)cm, 4¹/₄ (5:6¹/₄)in. Work 6 rows in garter stitch, every row knit. Cast off.

TO FINISH: Sew in all ends by weaving along the knitting, not up the side. Lay work out flat and steam gently. Sew side and sleeve seams, leaving the garter stitch band unsewn to form a little vent detail. Cut the length of cotton tape in half, fold under 1cm (¹/₂in) of one end of the tape and oversew onto one side of the back neck split. Repeat for other side. Tie tapes into a bow.

classic cashmere leggings

Although you see them less frequently nowadays, leggings are extremely useful in cold weather. They bring back memories of post-war babies and sepia-tinted photographs. These particular leggings are reworked in soft, luxurious cashmere, making them uniquely comfortable for your baby, although they could be equally easy knitted in merino wool or cotton. The leggings can be adjusted to fit at the waist with washed-cotton tapes threaded through eyelet holes. The feet to the leggings have attractive fully fashioned detailing. Combine them with the cashmere sweater (see page 20) and the bootees (see page 32), if you knit them without the feet, for a complete outfit.

how to make: **classic cashmere leggings**

opposite: These classic leggings are worked in softest cashmere, with delicate fashioned detailing, garter stitch feet and washed-cotton tape ties.

SIZING: For sizing refer to chart on page 112.

MATERIALS: 3 (3:4) x 25g balls 4 ply yarn, e.g. Jaeger cashmere (knits as medium) • Pair of 3.75mm (US 5) needles • Pair of 3.25mm (US 3) needles • Sewing needle • Cotton tape approximately 84 cm (33in) long

TENSION (GAUGE): 22 stitches and 32 rows to 10cm (4in) measured over stocking (stockinette) stitch using 3.75mm (US 5) needles.

TECHNIQUES: A few simple techniques are needed for these leggings. Increasing and decreasing, worked two stitches in from the edge, to give a fully fashioned look; knitting through the back of the loops, making an eyelet by taking the yarn over and picking up stitches. These are all explained in more detail on page 124.

METHOD: RIGHT LEG: start at waistline. Using 3.25mm (US 3) needles, cast on 58 (62:66) stitches and work 3 rows in rib as follows: Every row: knit 1 stitch, purl 1 stitch alternately to the end of the row.

MAKE EYELETS: Next row: knit 1 stitch, purl 1 stitch, ★ yarn over, purl 2 stitches together, knit 1 stitch, purl 1 stitch: repeat from ★ to the end of the row. Work 3 more rows in rib as set.
Change to 3.75mm (US 5) needles and stocking (stockinette) stitch. Then work as follows: **Row 1:** knit **Row 2:** purl.

WORK BACK SHAPING ROWS: Row 1: knit 10 (12:14) stitches, turn, purl 10 (12:14) stitches. **Row 2:** knit 16 (18:20) stitches, turn, purl 16 (18:20) stitches. **Row 3:** knit 22 (24:26) stitches, turn, purl 22 (24:26) stitches. Continue like this, working 6 extra stitches on

every row until the row knit 40 (42:44) stitches, turn, purl 40 (42:44) stitches has been worked. ★★ Continue to work in stocking (stockinette) stitch, across all the stitches. Increase at each end of the 5 (5:7)th row and then every following 10th row until there are 68 (72:76) stitches. Work straight, without any further shaping, until the front seam (the short edge of the work) measures 18 (20:23)cm/7 (8:9)in, ending with a purl row. Place coloured threads at each end of the last row.

SHAPE LEG: Row 1: knit 1 stitch, knit 2 stitches together through the back loops, knit to the last 3 stitches, knit 2 stitches together, knit 1 stitch. **Row 2:** purl 1 stitch, purl 2 stitches together, purl to last 3 stitches, purl 2 stitches together through the back loops, purl 1 stitch. Repeat these 2 rows twice more. *(56 (60:64) stitches)* Now decrease 1 stitch at each end of the next and every following third row until 28 (32:36) stitches remain. Work straight until leg measures 16 (18:20)cm/6 (7:8) in from the coloured markers, ending with a purl row. ★★

DIVIDE FOR THE FOOT: Knit 23 (26:29) stitches, turn. Purl 9 (9:11) stitches, turn. Work 14 (18:22) rows stocking (stockinette) stitch on these 9 (9: 11) stitches. Break yarn. With right side facing, rejoin the yarn to the inside edge of 14 (17: 18) stitches and pick up and knit 7 (9: 11) stitches along the side of the foot, knit across the 9 (9:11) stitches on the needle, pick up and knit 7 (9:11) stitches along the other side of the foot, knit across remaining 5 (6:7) stitches. *(42 (50:58) stitches)* Knit 7 (9:9) rows.

SHAPE FOOT: Row 1: knit 14 (18:22) stitches, knit 2 stitches together, knit 1 stitch, knit 2 stitches together, knit 16 (20:24) stitches, knit 2 stitches together, knit 1 stitch, knit 2 stitches together, knit 2 stitches.

left: Simple eyelets holes are worked by making an extra stitch and then knitting the next two stitches together. Cotton tape is then threaded through the holes and tied loosely at the front.

Row 2: knit. **Row 3:** knit 13 (17:21) stitches, knit 2 stitches together, knit 1 stitch, knit 2 stitches together, knit 14 (18:22) stitches, knit 2 stitches together, knit 1 stitch, knit 2 stitches together, knit 1 stitch. **Row 4:** knit. **Row 5:** knit 12 (16:20) stitches, knit 2 stitches together, knit 1 stitch, knit 2 stitches together, knit 12 (16:20) stitches, knit 2 stitches together, knit 1 stitch, knit 2 stitches together. Cast off.

LEFT LEG: Using 3.25mm (US 3) needles, cast on 58 (62:66) stitches and work rib and eyelets as for right leg. Change to 3.75mm (US 5) needles and work in stocking (stockinette) stitch as follows: **Next row:** knit.

WORK BACK SHAPING ROWS: **Row 1:** purl 10 (12:14) stitches, turn, knit 10 (12:14) stitches. **Row 2:** purl 16 (18:20) stitches, turn, knit 16 (18:20) stitches. **Row 3:** purl 22 (24:26) stitches, turn, knit 22 (24:26) stitches. Continue like this, working 6 extra stitches on every row until the row purl 40 (42:44) stitches, turn, knit 40 (42:44) stitches has been worked. **Next row:** purl to the end. Now work from ★★ to ★★ as on right leg.

DIVIDE FOR THE FOOT: knit 14 (17:18) stitches, turn. Purl 9 (9:11) stitches, turn.
Work 14 (18:22) rows in stocking (stockinette) stitch on these 9 (9: 11) stitches. Break yarn. With right side facing,

left: The leg seam and foot seam are joined in one straight continuous line. The garter stitch gives shape to the sole.

rejoin the yarn to the inside edge of 5 (6:7) stitches and pick up and knit 7 (9:11) stitches along the side of the foot, knit across 9 (9:11) stitches on the needle, pick up and knit 7 (9:11) stitches along the other side of the foot, knit across the remaining 14 (17:18) stitches. *(42 (50:58) stitches)* Knit 7 (9:9) rows.

SHAPE THE FOOT: Row 1: knit 2 stitches, knit 2 stitches together, knit 1 stitch, knit 2 stitches together, knit 16 (20:24) stitches, knit 2 stitches together, knit 1 stitch, knit 2 stitches together, knit 14 (18:22) stitches. **Row 2:** knit. **Row 3:** knit 1 stitch, knit 2 stitches together, knit 1 stitch, knit 2 stitches together, knit 14 (18:22) stitches, knit 2 stitches together, knit 1 stitch, knit 2 stitches together, knit 13 (17:21) stitches. **Row 4:** knit. **Row 5:** knit 2 stitches together, knit 1 stitch, knit 2 stitches together, knit 12 (16:20) stitches, knit 2 stitches together, knit 1 stitch, knit 2 stitches together, knit 12 (16:20) stitches. Cast off.

TO FINISH: Sew in all ends by weaving them along the knitting, not up the side. Lay work out flat and steam gently. With right sides together pin and sew the back and front seams to the markers, then sew up the inside leg and finally the foot seams, noting the seam is on the side of the foot. Thread tape through the eyelet holes, and tie in a bow.

classic cashmere bootees

These little bootees are ideal for both very young babies and those just beginning to get to their feet. Knitted in cashmere, they are soft and gentle on the delicate skin of the baby's feet, although they can be knitted in merino wool or cotton equally well. The simple roll edge gives the classic pattern a modern touch. The techniques required for these bootees are not difficult – you simply need to be able to pick up a few stitches. They make the perfect gift for a baby shower, and can be added to the sweater (see page 20) and the leggings (see page 26) if you knit the latter without the feet.

how to make: **classic cashmere bootees**

SIZING: For sizing refer to chart on page 112.

MATERIALS: 1 (1:1) x 25g ball 4 ply yarn, e.g. Jaeger cashmere (knits as medium) or Rowan wool/cotton • Pair of 3.75mm (US 5) needles • Safety pin

TENSION (GAUGE): 24 stitches and 32 rows to 10cm (4in) square measured over stocking (stockinette) stitch using 3.75mm (US 5) needles.

TECHNIQUES: For this project you need to be able to pick up stitches. An explanation of how to do so is given on page 124.

top left: Working on the centre set of stitches to make the top of the foot. A spare needle or large safety pins may be useful for holding the stitches not in use.

top right: Stitches along the sides and the edge are picked up and worked in garter stitch to make the sole.

METHOD: With 3.75mm (US 5) needles cast on 29 (33:37) stitches and work 10 (10:12) rows stocking (stockinette) stitch. **Next row:** knit 19 (22: 25) stitches, turn. **Next row:** purl 9 (11:13) stitches, turn. On 9 (11:13) stitches, work 14 (14:16) rows in stocking (stockinette) stitch. Break yarn. With right side of work facing, rejoin yarn to the inside edge of the 10 (11: 12) stitches and pick up and knit 7 (9: 11) stitches along the side of the foot, knit across 9 (11: 13) stitches on the needle, pick up and knit 7 (9:11) stitches along the other side of the foot, and finally knit across the remaining 10 (11:12) stitches. *(43 (51 :59) stitches)* Work 7 (9:11) rows of garter stitch, every row knit.

SHAPE THE FOOT: Row 1: knit 2 stitches, knit 2 stitches together, knit 15 (19:23) stitches, knit 2 stitches together, knit 1 stitch, knit 2 stitches together, knit 15 (19:23) stitches, knit 2 stitches together, knit 2 stitches. **Row 2:** knit. **Row 3:** knit 2 stitches, knit 2 stitches together, knit 13 (17:21) stitches, knit 2 stitches together, knit 1 stitch, knit 2 stitches together, knit 13 (17:21) stitches, knit 2 stitches together, knit 2 stitches. **Row 4:** knit. **Row 5:** knit 2 stitches, knit 2 stitches together, knit 11 (15:19) stitches, knit 2 stitches together, knit 1 stitch, knit 2 stitches together, knit 11 (15:19) stitches knit 2 stitches together, knit 2 stitches. Cast off.

TO MAKE UP: Weave in all ends along the work, not up the side as this will cause a lumpy edge. Lay work out and gently steam. Join the heel and the foot with a flat seam. Roll over the top edge and stitch down at the back seam with a single stitch to keep the roll edge in position.

below: A simple first gift for the new baby, these little bootees can be made in a night or even on the way to work. The simple roll edge gives a modern touch to a traditional bootee pattern. Knit them in cashmere or the finest merino wool for the ultimate in comfort for baby's tiny toes. Alternatively, make them in cotton for a summer arrival.

garter stitch cardigan

This is one of the simplest patterns of all, knitted in garter stitch in double knit yarn throughout, in one piece, with simple garter stitch bands at the front and the sleeve hems. The only technique involved is creating the simple buttonholes in the front bands. Five small, neat buttons fasten the cardigan, and the V-neck makes it very comfortable for the baby to wear. Knit it in cotton or wool, or a mixture of both, for all-year-round comfort.

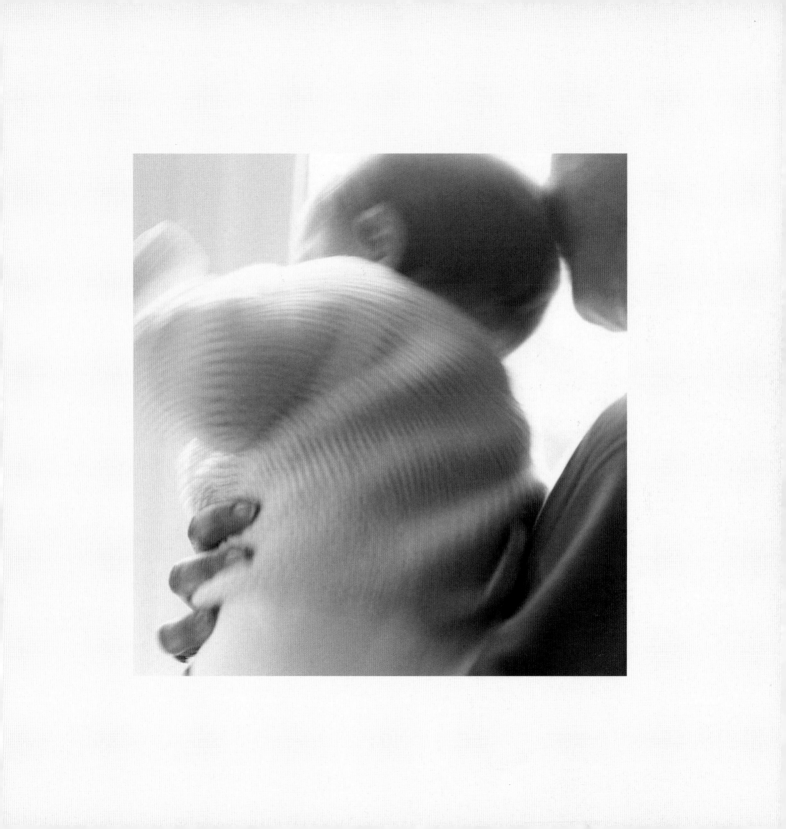

how to make: **garter stitch cardigan**

SIZE: For sizing refer to chart on page 113.

MATERIALS: 3 x 50g balls double knit yarn, e.g. Rowan wool/cotton or Rowan double knit cotton • Pair of 3.75mm (US 5) needles • Pair of 4mm (US 6) needles • 5 buttons • Stitch holder • Sewing needle

TENSION (GAUGE): 22 stitches and 36 rows to 10cm (4in) square measured over garter stitch using 4mm (US 6) needles.

TECHNIQUES: The special techniques are increasing and decreasing, and picking up stitches (see page 124).

METHOD: Using 3.75mm (US 5) needles, cast on 50 (56:62) stitches. Work 5 rows in garter stitch, every row knit. Change to 4mm (US 6) needles and continue until work measures 12 (13.5:15)cm/4^3/$_4$ (5^1/$_2$:6)in.

SHAPE SLEEVES: Cast on 17 (19:21) stitches at the beginning of the next 2 rows. *(84 (94:104) stitches)*

Continue until work measures 21 (23:25)cm/8^1/$_4$ (9:9^3/$_4$)in.

WORK RIGHT FRONT AND SLEEVE: Knit 30 (34:38) stitches, turn and leave remaining 54 (60:66) stitches on a stitch holder.
★ Working on 30 (34:38) stitches, knit 4 (4:6) rows straight, increase at neck edge on next and every alternate row until there are 41 (46:51) stitches on the needle. Continue straight until sleeve measures 18 (19:20)cm/7 (7^1/$_2$:8)in in depth, ending at sleeve edge. Cast off 17 (19:21) stitches and continue on the remaining 24 (27:30) stitches until work measures 41 (45:49)cm/16 (17^3/$_4$:19^1/$_4$)in. Change to 3.75 mm (US 5) needles, knit 5 rows. Cast off.

WORK LEFT FRONT AND SLEEVE: Place 24 (26:28) stitches on stitch holder for back neck. Rejoin the yarn to the remaining 30 (34:38) stitches at neck edge, and knit to the end of the row. Work from ★ to match the first side.

above left: Knitted in medium-weight yarn, such as merino wool or cotton, or a blend of both, this little cardigan is very quick and easy to make.

above right: The stitches are picked up along the fronts and the neck edge to give a neat finish and small eyelet buttonholes are made in the garter stitch band.

right: Fastened with tiny mother of pearl buttons and updated with three-quarter length sleeves, this garter stitch cardigan is a timeless and versatile favourite.

SLEEVE BANDS: With right side of work facing, using 3.75mm (US 5) needles, pick up 37 (41:45) stitches along the sleeve edge. Knit 4 rows. Cast off.

FRONT BAND: Using 3.75mm (US 5) needles and with right side of work facing, pick up 31 (35:39) stitches up right front, 15 (16: 19) stitches up right neck, 24 (26:28) stitches from stitch holder, 15 (16:18) stitches down left neck and 31 (35:39) stitches down left front. *(116 (128:144) stitches)* Knit 2 rows.

TO MAKE BUTTONHOLES: Knit to last 33 (37:41) stitches ★ yarn forward, knit 2 stitches together, knit 5(6:7) stitches, repeat from ★ three more times, yarn forward, knit 2 stitches together, knit to the end. Knit 1 row, then cast off.

TO MAKE UP: Weave in all ends. Lay work out flat and gently steam. With the right sides of the knitting facing, sew up the sleeve and side seams using simple overstitch, leaving the sides open 2.5cm (1in) at the bottom to make a vent detail. Sew on the buttons to correspond with the buttonholes.

personalized baby blanket

This wonderfully soft baby blanket, knitted in a very soft cotton blend, relies on its exquisite texture and classic design for its appeal. Knitted in stocking (stockinette) stitch, with a raised garter stitch border, it can be knitted quickly and easily by the most inexperienced knitter. To add character to the blanket, a monogrammed B for baby can be positioned in the centre of the blanket, by simply reversing the stitches from knit to purl to form the letter. If you prefer you could work the baby's initial instead. Charts for this purpose are given at the back of the book.

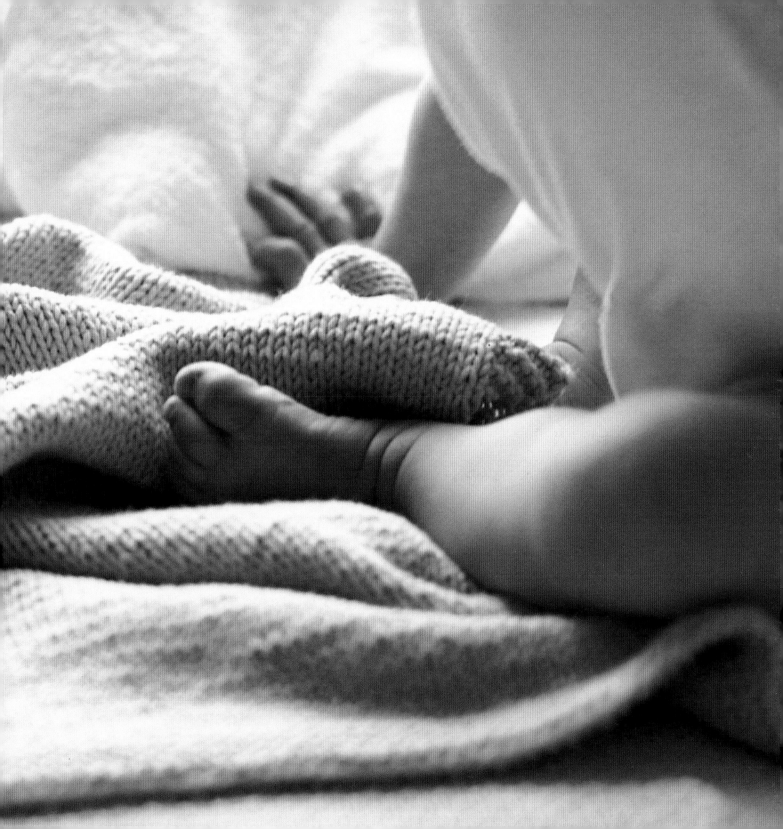

how to make: **personalized baby blanket**

SIZE: This blanket measures 90cm (36in) x 74cm (29in)

MATERIALS: 11 x 50g balls chunky yarn, e.g. Rowan all seasons cotton • Pair of 4.5mm (US 7) needles • Sewing needle

TENSION (GAUGE): 18 stitches and 25 rows to 10cm (4in) square measured over stocking (stockinette) stitch using 4.5mm (US 7) needles

TECHNIQUES: Always start a new ball of yarn at the beginning of a row, not in the middle. You need to follow the chart on page 116.

METHOD: With 4.5mm (US 7) needles cast on 130 stitches and work 7 rows in garter stitch, every row knit. Change to stocking (stockinette) stitch with garter stitch edges as follows: **Row 1:** knit all stitches. **Row 2:** knit 5 stitches, purl to the last 5 stitches, knit 5 stitches. Repeat rows 1 and 2 forty seven times. *(96 rows)*

above: A detail of the garter stitch border to the blanket, which helps to give it a solid, firm edge.

opposite: The initial B is created in the centre of the blanket by simply reversing stitches from knit to purl. It creates not only the letter itself, but an interesting texture to the surface. The heavier weight yarn knits up quickly, making this an easy yet effective project to make for the nursery or the stroller.

With the right side of the work facing you, work the letter 'B' for baby by referring to the 24 stitches and 32 rows from the chart on page 116. (Charts for other letters are given on the following pages.)
Row 1: knit 53 stitches; working from the chart for 'B', knit 5 stitches, purl 19 stitches; knit to the end. **Row 2:** knit 5 stitches, purl 48 stitches; working from the chart for 'B', knit 20 stitches, purl 4 stitches; purl to the last 5 stitches, knit 5 stitches. This places the letter in the centre of the blanket. Continue to work from the chart, working odd number rows from right to left and even number rows from left to right. When you have worked the letter chart, work another 95 rows in stocking (stockinette) stitch with garter stitch edges, ending with the wrong side facing you. Work 7 rows in garter stitch. Cast off.

TO FINISH: Sew in any loose ends. Gently steam and press the knitting flat.

personalized baby cushion

This is very simple and quick to knit in a mixture of stocking (stockinette) stitch

and garter stitch. Very similar to the baby blanket in design, the cushion

features a prominent initial in the centre, reversed out of the stocking

(stockinette) stitch. Charts for other initials are given at the back of the book.

This cushion is knitted in a chunky cotton blend that is both light and soft.

The simple garter stitch edging creates a smart finishing touch, as does the

simple garter stitch panel on the back opening.

how to make: personalized baby cushion

SIZE: This cushion measures 40cm (16in) square.

MATERIALS: 5 x 50g balls chunky yarn, e.g. Rowan all seasons cotton • Pair of 4.5mm (US 7) needles • Sewing needle • 40cm (16in) square cushion pad.

TENSION (GAUGE): 18 stitches x 25 rows to 10cm (4in) square measured over stocking (stockinette) stitch using 4.5mm (US 7) needles.

TECHNIQUES: Always start a new ball of yarn at beginning of a row, not in the middle. You need to follow the chart for the initial shown on page 116.

METHOD: With 4.5mm (US 7) needles cast on 72 stitches and work 7 rows in garter stitch, every row knit. Change to stocking (stockinette) stitch with garter stitch edges. **Row 1:** knit. **Row 2:** knit 5 stitches, purl to last 5 stitches, knit 5 stitches. Repeat rows 1 and 2 until work measures 27cm (10³/₄in), ending with a knit row. Change to garter stitch and work 7 rows. Change to stocking (stockinette) stitch with garter stitch edges as before and work 26 rows. With the right side of the knitting facing you, work the letter B for baby by referring to the 24 stitches and 32 rows from the chart

top left: Stitch the two layers together at each side using the same yarn, matching the ridges of the garter stitch to ensure a neat finish.

top right: The simple garter stitch band creates a firm and decorative edge for the centre back opening of the cushion and requires no fastening.

opposite: This little cushion makes a nice personal touch for the baby either in the nursery or for the stroller.

on page 116. **Row 1:** knit 24 stitches; working from the chart for 'B', knit 5 stitches, purl 19 stitches, then knit to end. **Row 2:** knit 5 stitches, purl 19 stitches; working from the chart for 'B', knit 20 stitches, purl 4 stitches; purl to last 5 stitches, knit 5 stitches. This places the letter in the centre of the cushion. Continue to work from the chart, working odd number rows from right to left and even number rows from left to right. When you have worked the letter chart, next work another 27 rows in stocking (stockinette) stitch with garter stitch edges, ending with the wrong side of the knitting facing you. Work 7 rows in garter stitch. Change to stocking (stockinette) stitch with garter stitch edges and work 40 rows. Work 7 rows in garter stitch. Cast off.

TO FINISH: Weave in all ends. Lay work out flat, steam and press gently. With the right side of the work facing, fold the work in towards the centre from the first horizontal garter stitch bands, stitch the two layers together at each side using the same yarn and mattress stitch (see page 124). Now fold knitting in from third horizontal garter stitch band and stitch the seams as before sewing through all the thickness of the overlapping pieces to make an 'envelope'. Turn right side out and place cushion pad inside.

chunky knit cardigan

This is another classic cardigan pattern for a baby, but given a modern twist thanks to chunky, quick-to-knit cotton yarn. Simple rib trims are used for the front button bands and for the sleeve hems, and the raglan sleeves have an unusual and attractive, fully fashioned decreasing detail. This simple cardigan can be knitted as an outfit with the beanie hat on page 54.

how to make : chunky knit cardigan

SIZING: For sizing refer to chart on page 113.

MATERIALS: 3 (3:4) x 50g balls chunky yarn, e.g. Rowan all seasons cotton • Pair of 4mm (US 6) needles • Pair of 4.5mm (US 7) needles • Sewing needle • 3 buttons • Safety pin

TENSION (GAUGE): 18 stitches and 25 rows to 10cm (4in) square measured over stocking (stockinette) stitch using 4.5mm (US 7) needles.

TECHNIQUES: The only special techniques involved are increasing and decreasing and knitting through the back of the loops (see page 124).

METHOD: BACK: Using 4mm (US 6) needles cast on 40 (44:50) stitches and work 2cm (1in) in simple rib stitch as follows: **Every row:** ★ knit 1 stitch, purl 1 stitch, repeat from ★ to end. Change to 4.5mm (US 7) needles and work in stocking (stockinette) stitch until knitting measures 9 (11:13)cm/3^1/$_2$(4^1/$_4$:5)in from the cast on edge.

top left: Heavier weight cotton yarn makes this a quick design to knit up and the roundness of the yarn gives clarity to the simple stitch.

top right: Knit the decrease stitches three stitches in from the edge. This will give a softer shape and a modern "fashioned" detail to this simple classic design.

opposite: This design can be worked in cotton or wool and be made for either girl or boy.

SHAPE ARMHOLES: Cast off 2 stitches at the beginning of the next 2 rows. **Next row:** knit 3 stitches, knit 2 stitches together, knit to the last 5 stitches, knit 2 stitches together through the back of the loops, knit to the end. Decrease 1 stitch at each end of the next 3 knit rows, in the same way. *(28:(32:38) stitches)* Continue straight until work measures 17 (19:22)cm/6^3/$_4$ (7^1/$_2$:8^3/$_4$)in.

SHAPE SHOULDERS: Cast off 7 (8:10) stitches at the beginning of the next 2 rows. Leave the remaining stitches on a safety pin to pick up later.

WORK LEFT FRONT: With 4mm (US 6) needles cast on 19 (21:24) stitches. Work 2cm (1in) in simple rib as on back. Change to 4.5mm (US 7) needles and work in stocking (stockinette) stitch until knitting measures 9(11:13) cm/3^1/$_2$ (4^1/$_4$: 5)in, ending with a purl row. ★★

SHAPE ARMHOLES: Cast off 2 stitches at the beginning the next row, knit to end. **Next row:** purl to the last 5 stitches, purl 2 stitches together, purl 3 stitches. Now decrease 1 stitch on each purl row 3 more times in this same way. *(13 (15: 18) stitches)*

SHAPE NECK (RIGHT SIDE FACING): **Row 1:** knit to last 5 stitches, knit 2 stitches together, knit 3 stitches. **Row 2:** purl 3 stitches, purl 2 stitches together, purl to end. **Row 3:** as row 1. **Row 4:** purl. Repeat rows 3 and 4 until 7 (8: 10) stitches remain. Continue without shaping until work measures 17 (19:22)cm/6³/₄ (7¹/₂:8³/₄)in, ending with a purl row. Cast off.

WORK RIGHT FRONT: Work as the left front to ★★.

SHAPE ARMHOLES: **Row 1:** knit. **Row 2:** cast off 2 stitches, purl to end. **Row 3:** knit to last 5 stitches, knit 2 stitches together through the back of the loops, knit 3 stitches. **Row 4:** purl. **Rows 5–8:** repeat rows 3 and 4 twice more. *(14 (16: 19) stitches)* **Row 9:** knit 3 stitches, knit 2 stitches together through the back loops, knit to last 5 stitches, knit 2

stitches together through the back loops, knit 3 stitches. **Row 10:** purl to the last 5 stitches, purl 2 stitches together through the back loops, purl 3 stitches. Continue decreasing on neck edge only as set on each knit row until 7 (8:10) stitches remain. Continue without shaping until work measures 17 (19:22)cm/6³/₄ (7¹/₂:8³/₄)in, ending with a purl row. Cast off.

SLEEVES: *Make 2 the same.* With 4mm (US 6) needles cast on 23 (25:27) stitches. Work 2cm (1in) in simple rib stitch as on back. Change to 4.5mm (US 7) needles and stocking (stockinette) stitch. Increase 1 stitch at each end of the first row and every 6th row that follows to 29 (31:33) stitches. Continue straight until the knitting measures 12.5 (15:18)cm/5 (6:7)in.

SHAPE TOP: Cast off 2 stitches at the beginning of the next 2 rows. **Row 1:** knit 3 stitches, knit 2 stitches together, knit to the last 5 stitches, knit 2 stitches together through the back of the loops, knit 3 stitches. **Row 2:** purl. Repeat rows 1 and 2 until 17 (19:21) stitches remain. Cast off 3 stitches at the beginning of the next 4 rows. *(5 (7:9) stitches)* Cast off.

TO MAKE UP: Sew in all ends. Lay pieces out flat and steam and press gently. From the right side of the work join shoulder seams taking one stitch from the back and one from the front alternately.

FRONT BAND: With 4mm (US 6) needles and the right side of the knitting facing you, pick up and knit 20 (22:25) stitches up the right front, 13 (14: 15) stitches up the V-slope, 14 (16: 18) stitches from safety pin, 13 (14: 15) stitches down the V-slope, 20 (22:25) stitches down the left front. *(82 (92:102) stitches)* Work 2 rows knit 1 stitch, purl 1 stitch rib. **Next row:** make 3 buttonholes as follows: Rib 2 stitches ★ yarn over, purl 2 stitches together, rib 6 (8:10) stitches. Repeat from ★ twice more, rib to the end. Work 1 more row in rib. Then cast off.

TO FINISH: Set the sleeves in between the armhole shapings. Stitch in place. Sew the sleeve and side seams. Sew on the 3 buttons to correspond with the buttonholes.

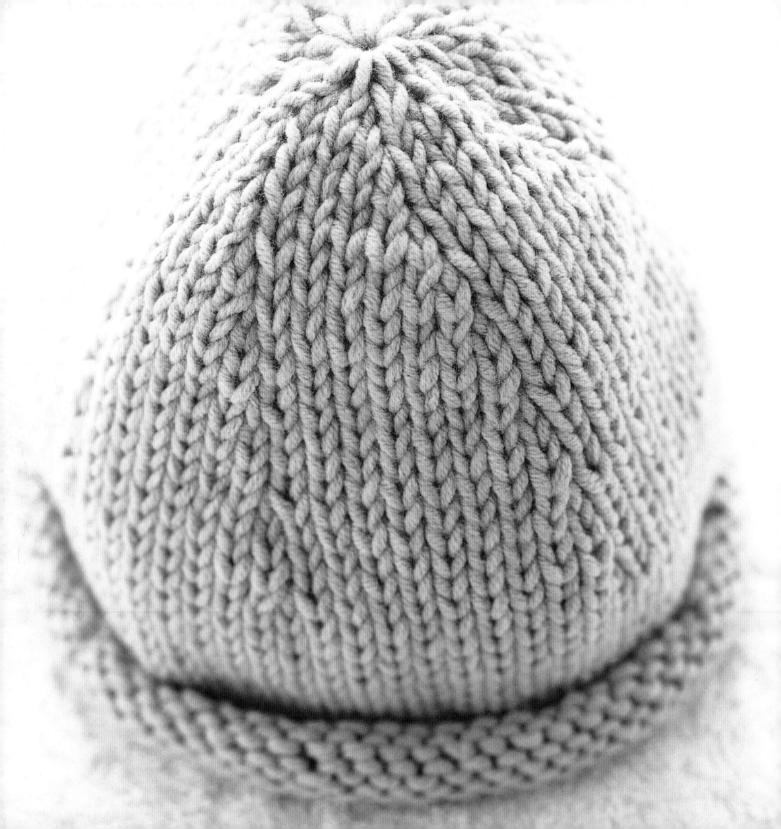

baby's beanie hat

This little pull-on hat is very quick and easy to knit. If you knit it in the same chunky cotton yarn as the cardigan on page 50 it makes an attractive outfit for the baby. The simple roll-edged brim allows you to adjust the size to fit the baby's head, and the stocking (stockinette) stitch and simple shaping are very easy to work. The hat is knitted on two needles, with a back seam.

how to make : **baby's beanie hat**

opposite: This is easily and quickly knitted in stocking (stockinette) stitch on two needles. Use a size smaller needle to cast on to give a neater roll edge. The shaping is created by knitting two stitches together at intervals on the knit rows.

SIZING: For sizing refer to chart on page 113.

MATERIALS: 1 (1:1) x 50g ball chunky yarn, e.g. Rowan all seasons cotton • Pair of 4mm (US 6) needles • Pair of 4.5mm (US 7) needles • Sewing needle

TENSION (GAUGE): 18 stitches and 25 rows to 10cm (4in) square measured over stocking (stockinette) stitch using 4.5mm (US 7) needles.

TECHNIQUES: No special techniques required.

METHOD: With 4mm (US 6) needles, cast on 61 (68:75) stitches and work 4 rows in stocking (stockinette) stitch. Change to 4.5mm (US 7) needles and work 16 (18:20) rows in stocking (stockinette) stitch. Now decrease as follows: **Decrease row 1:** ★ knit 8 stitches, knit 2 stitches together, repeat from ★ to last 1 (8:5) stitches, knit 1 (8:5) stitches. Work 3 rows in stocking (stockinette) stitch. **Decrease row 2:** ★ knit 7 stitches, knit 2 stitches together, repeat from ★ to last 1 (8:5) stitches, knit 1 (8:5) stitches. Work 3 rows in stocking (stockinette) stitch. **Decrease row 3:** ★ knit 6 stitches, knit 2 stitches together, repeat from ★ to last 1 (0:5) stitches, knit 1 (0:5) stitches. Work 3 rows in stocking (stockinette) stitch. **Decrease row 4:** ★ knit 5 stitches, knit 2 stitches together, repeat from ★ to last 1 (0:5) stitches, knit 1 (0:5) stitches. Purl 1 row. **Decrease row 5:** ★ knit 4 stitches, knit 2 stitches together, repeat from ★ to last 1 (0:5) stitches, knit 1 (0:5) stitches. Purl 1 row. **Decrease row 6:** ★ knit 3 stitches, knit 2 stitches together, repeat from ★ to last 1 (0:0) stitch, knit 1 (0:0) stitch. Purl 1 row. **Decrease row 7:** ★ knit 2 stitches, knit 2 stitches together, repeat from ★ to last 1 (0:0) stitch, knit 1 (0:0) stitch. Purl 1 row. **Decrease row 8:** knit 2 stitches together across row to last 1 (1:0) stitch, knit 1 (1:0). Leave length of yarn (for sewing) and break yarn.
With the wrong side of the work facing you, thread yarn through the remaining stitches, pull up and sew to secure.

TO FINISH: Sew the seam. Gently steam and roll brim to required length, and catch down at back to secure the brim into position.

garter stitch wrap top

This exquisitely simple wrap top is ideal for a new baby. It is knitted

in silk, which is wonderfully soft for the baby to snuggle into and

exactly the right choice of yarn for a new baby's delicate and

sensitive skin. You can knit it in white, or in light silvery grey or a

muted soft pink. Match it with a pair of the silk slippers (see page

80) for an heirloom gift for a new baby or as a present for a special

celebration. Organza ribbons, fastened at the back, keep the top

snugly in place.

how to make : garter stitch wrap top

SIZING: For sizing refer to chart on page 114.

MATERIALS: 1 (2:2) x 50g balls fine yarn, e.g. Jaeger 4 ply silk, Jaeger Siena 100% cotton or Rowan true 4 ply botany • Pair of 3mm (US 2) needles • Sewing needle • Organza ribbon, 1cm (¹/₂in) wide and 60cm (24in) long.

TENSION (GAUGE): 28 stitches and 48 rows to 10cm (4in) square measured over garter stitch using 3mm (US 2) needles.

TECHNIQUES: Slip the first stitch and knit the last stitch of every row to give a neat edge. Work the cast on edge with a size smaller needle to give a neat firm edge. The only other special technique needed is increasing (see page 124).

METHOD: This garment is made in one piece, starting at the back hemline. Using 3mm (US 2) needles, cast on 49 (55:61) stitches and work 48 (54:60) rows in garter stitch (every row: slip the first stitch, knit to the end).

SHAPE SLEEVES: Cast on 7 (11:15) stitches at the beginning of the next 2 rows. *(63 (77:91) stitches)* Work a further 28 (34:40) rows in garter stitch.

SHAPE NECK: Next row: slip the first stitch, knit 21 (27:33) stitches, cast off 19 (21:23) stitches, knit to end.

SHAPE LEFT FRONT: Working on first set of 22 (28:34) stitches, knit 8 rows, ending at the sleeve edge. **Row 9:** knit to the last 3 stitches, increase in the next stitch, knit 2 stitches. **Row 10:** knit 1 stitch, increase in the next stitch, knit to the end. Repeat rows 9 and 10 until you have 44 (56:68) stitches, ending at the sleeve edge. **Next row:** cast off 7 (11: 15) stitches, knit to the last 3 stitches, increase in the next stitch, knit 2 stitches. Continue increasing at the neck edge as before until you have 49 (55:61) stitches. Knit a further 38 (46:54) rows without shaping. Cast off.

SHAPE RIGHT FRONT: Rejoin yarn to remaining 22 (28:34) stitches at the neck edge and knit 8 rows, ending at the neck edge. **Row 9:** knit 1 stitch, increase in the next stitch, knit to the end. **Row 10:** slip the first stitch, knit to the last 3 stitches, increase in the next stitch, knit 2 stitches. Repeat rows 9 and 10 until you have 43 (55:67) stitches, ending at the sleeve edge. **Next row:** cast off 7 (11:15) stitches, knit to the last 3 stitches, increase in the next stitch, knit 2 stitches. Continue increasing at the neck edge as before until you have 49 (55:61) stitches. Knit a further 38 (46:54) rows without shaping. Cast off.

TO FINISH: Weave in all ends, along the fabric not up the side edge. Lay work out flat and gently steam. Cut the length of ribbon in half and sew the ribbon onto each front below the shaped edge. Join left side and sleeve seam. Join right side and sleeve seam, leaving a small opening to match the ribbon position of left front.

TO FASTEN: Cross right front over left front and thread ribbon on left front through opening. Tie at the back.

opposite: This simple kimono-shaped wrap top is knitted in one piece in easy garter stitch. A small hole is left in one side seam just below the armhole for the ribbon to pass through when the vest is wrapped over. The ribbons must be securely tied at the back, out of the baby's reach. Alternatively, secure the kimono with a button and loop fastening.

cashmere teddy bear

This really simple teddy bear is a gift to cherish. It is constructed like a sweater with a back, front, sleeves (as arms), and a head knitted in one piece, and two little ears. The wonderfully soft yarn makes it an instant favourite for any baby to cuddle. Once knitted, it is simply stitched and filled with soft stuffing. A simple chart (on page 123) shows you where to increase and decrease. The teddy's face is embroidered in satin stitch. You can personalize it in any way you choose. A cotton bow under the chin provides the finishing touch.

top left: This charming first teddy is knitted in four simple pieces (three of them twice).

top right: Once the torso, arms and legs are knitted and sewn together, the head can be sewn together too. The parts are then turned right sides out, and the body and head stuffed and finally sewn together.

right: The face is embroidered onto the teddy with thick black yarn. Sew French knots for the eyes and satin or long stitches for the nose and mouth. To finish, tie a ribbon around the neck.

how to make : **cashmere teddy bear**

SIZE: Height: 15cm (6in).

MATERIALS: 1 x 50g ball 4 ply yarn, e.g. Jaeger cashmere • Pair of 3.25mm (US 3) needles • Black embroidery thread • Safety pin • Ribbon • Filling/stuffing (washable)

TENSION (GAUGE): 26 stitches and 36 rows to 10cm (4in) square measured over stocking (stockinette) stitch using 3.25mm (US 3) needles.

TECHNIQUES: The only special techniques required are simple increasing and decreasing, and reading a chart (see page 124).

METHOD: Work in stocking (stockinette) stitch for all pieces. Charts for all parts are on page 123.

FRONT: FIRST LEG: Using 3.25mm (US 5) needles, cast on 6 stitches and knit 1 row. Increase 1 stitch at each end of the next 2 rows. ★ **Row 4:** increase 1 stitch at the beginning of the row, purl to the end. Work 3 rows. **Row 8:** purl, increase 1 stitch at the end of the row. 12 stitches. Work 4 rows. Break yarn and leave the stitches on a safety pin.

SECOND LEG: Work as for first leg to ★. **Row 4:** purl, increase 1 stitch at the end of the row. Work 3 rows. **Row 8:** increase 1 stitch at the beginning of the row, purl to the end. Work 4 rows. **Row 13:** knit 12 stitches, cast on 2 stitches, knit across 12 stitches from first leg.

BODY: Continue in stocking (stockinette) stitch until the work measures 8cm (3$^{1}/_{4}$in) from his toes, ending with a purl row. Shape for the arms by decreasing 1 stitch at each end of the next and every following third row until 18 stitches remain. Work 2 more rows. Cast off.

BACK: Work as for front of teddy bear.

THE ARMS: *Make 2.* Using 3.25mm (US 3) needles, cast on 14 stitches. Knit 1 row. Increase 1 stitch at each end of the next 3 rows. *(20 stitches)* Work 11 rows. Decrease 1 stitch at each end of the next 8 rows. Cast off the remaining 4 stitches.

THE EARS: *Make 2.* Using 3.25mm (US 3) needles, cast on 3 stitches and knit 1 row. Increase 1 stitch at each end of the next 3 rows. *(9 stitches)* Work 5 rows. Decrease 1 stitch at each end of the next 3 rows. *(3 stitches)* Cast off.

THE HEAD: Using 3.25mm (US 3) needles, cast on 36 stitches and work 2 rows. Increase 1 stitch at each end of the next 7 rows. *(50 stitches)* Purl 1 row. Decrease 1 stitch at each end of the next 13 rows. *(24 stitches)* Purl 1 row. Decrease 1 stitch at each end of the next and every alternate row until 8 stitches remain. Decrease 1 stitch at each end of the next 2 rows. Cast off the remaining 4 stitches.

TO MAKE UP: Lay the pieces out flat, and steam gently. With right sides of the fabric together, sew the sloping end of the arms to the armholes of the 2 body pieces. Leave the neck open. Starting with one arm, using a fine backstitch, sew around "hand", arm, body, both legs and back to the other "hand". Turn right side out. Stuff with filling. Make up head. Pin cast on edge into a circle and B to C (see chart on page 123). Sew seam. Pin point A to seam at BC to make nose. Stitch seam D-nose-D. Turn right side out. Stuff the head. Attach the head to the body, by oversewing neatly. Mould the head to suit, and characterize. Fold each ear in half, and over sew together. Attach to the head. Embroider 2 eyes with French knots. Embroider the nose in the shape of a triangle, then stitch 2 lines from the base of the nose for the mouth. Finally tie a ribbon around the neck.

vintage cardigan

A classic edge-to-edge cardigan pattern in stocking (stockinette) stitch finds a new lease of life knitted in 4-ply botany wool with an attractive velvet ribbon trim, bordering the neck, fronts and hem. Simple roll back cuffs add a practical finishing touch, allowing room for the baby to grow. Make it in muted art shades, like the soft violet colour shown here.

how to make : **vintage cardigan**

above left: The ribbon trim is attached all around the edge of the cardigan, inside the garter stitch border. The ribbon should be mitred at the corners for neatness.

above right: A cuff detail, the rolled back sleeve revealing the garter stitch reverse side. of the knitting.

opposite: This edge-to-edge cardigan is knitted in fine wool and takes its inspiration from knitting patterns of the past. Team it with the little ribbon-tied vest on page 90 to make a twinset.

SIZING: For sizing refer to chart on page 114.

MATERIALS: 3 (3:3) x 50g balls Rowan true 4 ply botany wool • Pair of 3.25mm (US 3) needles • 3 safety pins • Sewing needle • Velvet ribbon, approximately 110 (120:130)cm/43 (47:50)in long, or trim of choice.

TENSION (GAUGE): 28 stitches and 36 rows to 10cm (4in) square over stocking (stockinette) stitch using 3.25mm (US 3) needles.

TECHNIQUES: Simple increasing and decreasing are the only special techniques needed for this pattern (see explanation on page 124).

METHOD: BACK: Using 3.25mm (US 3) needles, cast on 67 (75:83) stitches and knit 3 rows. Right side of work facing, change to stocking (stockinette) stitch and continue until work measures 13 (15:16)cm/5 (6:6½)in.

SHAPE ARMHOLES: Cast off 4 stitches at the beginning of the next 2 rows. Decrease 1 stitch at each end of the next 6 rows. *(47 (55:63) stitches)* Continue until work measures 20 (23:26)cm/8 (9:10)in. Cast off 12 (15:18) stitches at the beginning of the next 2 rows. Break yarn and slip remaining 23 (25:27) stitches onto a safety pin.

RIGHT FRONT: Using 3.25mm (US 3) needles, cast on 34 (38:42) stitches and knit 3 rows. Right side of work facing, change to stocking (stockinette) stitch with garter stitch edge as follows: **Row 1:** knit. **Row 2:** purl to last 3 stitches, knit 3 stitches. Repeat these 2 rows until work measures 13 (15: 16)cm/5 (6:6½)in, ending with row 1.

SHAPE ARMHOLES: Cast off 4 stitches, purl to last 3 stitches, knit 3 stitches. Decrease 1 stitch at armhole edge on the next 6 rows. *(24 (28:32) stitches)* Then continue, without shaping, until the work measures 18 (20:22)cm/ 7 (7¾:8¾)in, ending with a knit row.

SHAPE NECK: Purl to last 6 (7:8) stitches, then slip these 6 (7:8) stitches onto a safety pin. Continue in stocking (stockinette) stitch, decreasing 1 stitch at the neck edge on the next 6 rows. *(12 (15:18) stitches)* Continue until work measures 20 (23:26)cm/8 (9:10)in, ending with a purl row. Cast off.

LEFT FRONT: Using 3.25mm (US 3) needles, cast on 34 (38:42) stitches and knit 3 rows. Right side of work facing, change to stocking (stockinette) stitch with garter stitch edge as follows: **Row 1:** knit. **Row 2:** knit 3 stitches, purl to the end of the row. Repeat these 2 rows until the work measures 13 (15:16)cm/5 (6:6½)in, ending with row 2.

SHAPE ARMHOLE: Cast off 4 stitches, knit to end of row. Decrease 1 stitch at armhole edge on the next 6 rows. *(24 (28:32) stitches)* Continue without shaping until work measures 18 (20:22)cm/7 (7¾:8¾)in, ending with a purl row.

SHAPE NECK: Knit to last 6 (7:8) stitches and then slip these 6 (7:8) stitches onto a safety pin. Continue in stocking (stockinette) stitch, decreasing 1 stitch at neck edge on the next 6 rows. *12 (15:18) stitches.* Continue until work measures 20 (23:26)cm, 8 (9: 10)in, ending with a purl row. Cast off.

NECKBAND: Sew shoulder seams. With right side facing, join yarn to the right front edge and knit across 6 (7:8) stitches on the safety pin, pick up and knit 12 (14:14) stitches to the shoulder, knit across 23 (25:27) stitches of the back neck, pick up and knit 12 (14:14) stitches down to the left front edge and knit across the last 6 (7:8) stitches on safety pin. *(59 (65:71) stitches)* Knit 2 rows. Cast off.

opposite: You may wish to make little slippers to co-ordinate with the vintage style cardigan. These ones are knitted in fine wool and trimmed in the same decorative ribbon. Refer to the instructions for the silk slippers (page 82) and simply change the yarn.

SLEEVES: Using 3.25mm (US 3) needles, cast on 36 (36:40) stitches and work in garter stitch for 4 (4:5)cm/1½ (1½:2)in. Change to stocking (stockinette) stitch, increasing 1 stitch at each end of every 6th row, until the sleeve measures 14 (17:19)cm/5½ (6½:7½)in.

SHAPE SLEEVEHEAD: Knit 2 stitches together at the beginning of the next 10 rows. Cast off.

TO FINISH: Sew in any loose ends. Lay the work out flat, pin out pieces and gently steam. Sew the sleeveheads into the armholes between shapings. Sew the side and sleeve seams. Turn up cuff.

TO DECORATE: Starting at the right side seam, pin the ribbon above the garter stitch hem, across the bottom of the back and left front; up the left front, around the neck, down the right front and across the front to the side seam. Sew into position with fine stitches.

sssh! baby sleeping cushion

This little cushion can be used to hang on the nursery or bedroom door to warn the household that the baby is asleep and must not be disturbed. One of the easiest projects in the book to make, it is an ideal gift for a first baby. It is knitted here in silk but could easily be made from cotton. The two little stocking (stockinette) stitch squares are simply stitched together and stuffed. The front is embroidered in cross stitch (see chart on page 123). Embroider the words and add an X for a loving kiss, or, if you prefer, embroider the baby's name or initials.

how to make: **sssh! baby sleeping cushion**

above right: Follow the chart given on page 123 to work the embroidery as shown, or personalize it with the baby's name or a little message of your choice.

opposite: A simple gift for a baby shower, this little cushion can be embroidered in pink or blue, to be hung on the nursery door to warn others not to disturb the baby while he or she is sleeping.

SIZE: This cushion measures approximately 13cm (5in) square.

MATERIALS: 1 x 50g ball fine yarn, e.g Jaeger 4 ply silk or Jaeger Siena cotton • Pair of 2mm (US 1) needles • Embroidery thread • Silk or synthetic ribbon, approximately 1m (39in) long x 1cm ($^1/_2$in) wide • Sewing needle • Silk or satin fabric, measuring approximately 15cm x 28cm (6in x 11in), for the cushion • Suitable stuffing for the cushion.

TENSION (GAUGE): 36 stitches and 46 rows to 10cm (4in) square measured over stocking (stockinette) stitch using 2mm (US 1) needles.

TECHNIQUES: Slip the first stitch and knit the last stitch of every row to give a neat edge. You will need to refer to the chart on page 123.

METHOD: Using 2mm (US 1) needles, cast on 44 stitches and work in stocking (stockinette) stitch for 56 rows. Cast off. Make a second piece to match.

TO EMBROIDER: Follow the chart given on page 123. Work in cross stitch.

TO MAKE UP: Lay the work out flat and press gently on the wrong side. Sew three sides.

TO MAKE THE PAD: Fold the fabric in half lengthways and sew the 2 side seams. Turn it right sides out and then stuff with filling and sew up the remaining edge. Insert the pad into the knitted square, and carefully sew the remaining seam.

TO FINISH: Cut a 36cm (14in) length of the ribbon. Attach this length of ribbon as a handle to the top of the cushion from the left corner to the right corner. Cut the remaining length of ribbon in half and tie into 2 bows and sew one to each top corner of the cushion.

lace-edged cuddle blanket

This classic baby blanket can be used in the pram, the cot or the car. Whether you knit it in white or in soft washed pastel shades, it is a timeless classic that will probably be handed down from baby to baby. Although it takes a little time to knit, the blanket is easy because it is knitted in sections made from stocking (stockinette) stitch and reverse stocking (stockinette) stitch, while the lace edging is knitted in four strips that are then joined together to edge the blanket. This particular blanket was knitted in cool natural cotton, but a warmer blanket could be worked in soft, luxurious merino wool.

how to make: **lace-edged cuddle blanket**

SIZE: This blanket measures approximately 110cm (43³/₄in) square.

MATERIALS: 17 x 50g balls fine cotton, e.g. Rowan Cotton Glace • Pair of 3.25mm (US 3) needles • Sewing needle

TENSION (GAUGE): 23 stitches and 32 rows to 10cm (4in) square measured over stocking (stockinette) stitch using 3.25mm (US 3) needles.

TECHNIQUES: Slip the first and knit the last stitch of every row to give a firm edge. "Yarn round needle" means bring yarn to the front of work (as if to purl a stitch) and take over the needle to the back, so making a stitch. "Yarn twice round needle" means bring yarn to the front of work, wind around needle twice, so making 2 stitches.

METHOD: Using 3.25mm (US 3) needles, cast on 60 stitches and work in stocking (stockinette) stitch until work measures 26cm (10¹/₄in), approximately 84 rows. Cast off. This makes one square. Make a total of 16 squares.

TO MAKE UP: Sew in all ends by weaving along the knitting not along the edge. Lay each square out flat and gently steam. Next layout the 16 squares in a grid of 4 squares wide by 4 squares deep, alternating right and wrong sides to make a pattern. Pin the squares together and oversew the edges.

LACE EDGING: This edging is worked lengthwise. Due to the nature of the pattern the number of stitches varies on some rows. Using 3.25mm (US 3) needles, cast on 10 stitches. Work as follows: **Row 1:** (right side) knit 3 stitches, ★ yarn round needle, knit 2 stitches together ★. Repeat ★ to ★, yarn twice round needle, knit 2 stitches together, knit 1 stitch *(11 stitches)* **Row 2:** knit 3 stitches, purl 1 stitch, knit 2 stitches, ★ yarn round needle, knit 2 stitches together ★. Repeat ★ to ★, knit 1 stitch. **Row 3:** knit 3 stitches, ★ yarn round needle, knit 2 stitches together ★. Repeat ★ to ★, knit 1 stitch, yarn twice round needle, knit 2 stitches together, knit 1 stitch. *(12 stitches)* **Row 4:** knit 3 stitches, purl 1 stitch, knit 3 stitches, ★ yarn round needle, knit 2 stitches together ★. Repeat ★ to ★, knit 1 stitch. **Row 5:** knit 3 stitches, ★ yarn round needle, knit 2 stitches together ★. Repeat ★ to ★, knit 2 stitches, yarn twice round needle, knit 2 stitches together, knit 1 stitch *(13 stitches)* **Row 6:** knit 3 stitches, purl 1 stitch, knit 4 stitches, ★ yarn round needle, knit 2 stitches together ★. Repeat ★ to ★, knit 1 stitch. **Row 7:** knit 3 stitches, ★ yarn round needle, knit 2 stitches together ★. Repeat ★ to ★, knit 6 stitches. **Row 8:** cast off 3 stitches, knit S stitches (1 stitch already on right needle) ★ yarn round needle, knit 2 stitches together ★. Repeat ★ to ★, knit 1 stitch. *(10 stitches)* Repeat these 8 rows until work, when slightly stretched, measures 110cm (43¹/₄in), ending with row 8. Cast off. Make 4 strips of lace in total.

TO FINISH: Sew in all ends by weaving along the knitting, not up the side. Pin a strip of lace edging to one side of the blanket so that the strip extends 3cm ($1^1/_4$in) over one end. Pin the second strip in place all along next side, sewing one end to overlap and letting strip extend 3cm ($1^1/_4$in) over other end. Sew on third and fourth strips in the same way. Taking care to ease corners to continue the scallop effect, lay work out flat and steam gently.

opposite left: Alternate the right and wrong sides of the knitted squares to make a patchwork effect.

opposite centre: Pin a strip of lace edging all along one side of the blanket, easing it as you do, and extending it over the corner of the blanket. Then sew into position.

opposite right: The second, third and fourth strips are sewn in the same way

left: The finished lace-edged blanket.

garter stitch silk slippers

Knitted in the very simplest garter stitch in fine silk, these delicate little slippers are the ideal gift for a new born baby, particularly when decorated with a rosebud trim or matching organza ribbons. Soft, stretchy and snug, they can be knitted in three sizes for babies from birth to nine months old. Only very simple shaping is needed, and the slippers can be knitted up in a few hours.

how to make: garter stitch silk slippers

SIZING: For sizing refer to chart on page 114.

MATERIALS: 1 x 50g ball 4 ply silk, e.g. Jaeger 4 ply silk • Pair of 2.75mm (US 2) needles • Sewing needle • Organza ribbon 1cm (¹/₂in) wide x 124cm (49in) long

TENSION (GAUGE): 28 stitches and 48 rows to 10cm square measured over garter stitch using 2.75mm (US 2) needles.

TECHNIQUES: Only simple increasing and decreasing are needed for this pattern (see explanation on page 124).

METHOD: Using 2.75mm (US 2) needles cast on 12 (16:20) stitches and work in garter stitch, every row knit. Increase 1 stitch at each end of the first and every alternate row until 24 (28:32) stitches are on the needle. Knit 2 rows without shaping. Decrease 1 stitch at each end of the first and every following alternate row until

above left: Each slipper is knitted in one piece, with very simple shaping.

above centre: The finished slipper before being stitched up.

above right: The untrimmed slippers, showing the simple shape used. When making up each slipper, sew the heel seam first and then join the sole to the upper, easing in any fullness.

opposite: Matching organza ribbon is stitched to the slippers at the heel seam as a finishing touch.

12 (16:20) stitches remain. You have now knitted the sole of the slipper. Cast on 7 stitches for the heel at the end of the last row. *(19 (23:27) stitches)* Continue on these stitches, keeping the heel edge straight, increasing 1 stitch at the toe edge on every alternate row until there are 25 (29:33) stitches on the needle, ending at heel edge. Cast off 12 (15: 18) stitches at the heel, knit to the end. Knit 13 (15:17) rows. Cast on 12 (15:18) stitches at the (heel) end of the last row. *(25 (29:33) stitches)* Keeping the heel edge straight decrease 1 stitch at the toe edge on every alternate row until 19 (23:27) stitches remain. Cast off.

TO FINISH: Sew in any loose ends. Join the straight seam at heel. Join the sole to the top of the slipper, easing the fullness around the toe. Cut length of ribbon in half. Then fold one length of the organza ribbon in half and sew it to the centre back of the slipper. Alternatively, personalize with embellishment of your choice.

traditional mabel dress

This delightful dress for small girls has nostalgic appeal, particularly if knitted in dusty pink or soft mauve. Worked in stocking (stockinette) stitch, the dress is gathered onto a simple yolk with a tiny picot edging detail at the neck. Knit it in soft fine cotton for summer, or in cashmere for winter. Fine organza ribbon ties the back of the dress at the neck, with a simple centre slit opening that slides easily over the baby's head. A simple garter stitch hem gives body to the base of the skirt.

how to make: **traditional mabel dress**

right: This simple little dress, with its yoke and decorative picot edging, is worked in fine 4 ply mercerized cotton, which gives an attractive sheen and a touch of nostalgia to this timeless design

SIZING: For sizing refer to chart on page 115.

MATERIALS: 3 (3:4) x 50g balls fine yarn e.g. Jaeger Siena 100% mercerized cotton • 2 pairs of 2.75mm (US 2) needles • Pair of 2.25mm (US 1) needles • Ribbon, approximately 84cm (33in) long and 1cm (^{1}/$_2$in) wide • Sewing needle

TENSION (GAUGE): 30 stitches and 38 rows to 10cm (4in) square measured over stocking (stockinette) stitch using 2.75mm (US 2) needles.

TECHNIQUES: Just a few special techniques are needed. Increasing and decreasing, knitting through the back of the loops and making a stitch without leaving a hole (up 1 stitch). See page 124 for explanations.

METHOD: BACK: Using 2.75mm (US 2) needles, cast on 125 (131:137) stitches and work 5 rows in garter stitch, every row: knit.
Change to stocking (stockinette) stitch and continue until work measures 19 (22:25)cm/7^1/$_2$ (8^3/$_4$:10)in, ending with a purl row.

BACK OPENING: Next row: knit 62 (65:68) stitches, cast off 1 stitch, knit 62 (65:68) stitches. Now work on the second set of stitches, knitting the last stitch of all purl rows to give a neat edge to the back opening. Continue in stocking (stockinette) stitch until work measures 22 (25:28)cm/8^1/$_2$ (10:11)in, ending with a knit row.

SHAPE ARMHOLE: Row 1: cast off 2 stitches, purl to the last stitch, knit 1 stitch. **Row 2:** knit to the last 4 stitches, knit 2 stitches together through the back loops, knit 2 stitches. **Row 3:** purl to the last stitch knit 1 stitch. Repeat rows 2 and 3 three times. *(56 (59:62) stitches)* ★★ **Decrease row:** knit 2 stitches together 28 (29:31) times, knit 0 (1:0) stitch. *(28 (30:31) stitches)* Knit 3 rows to mark back yoke. Continue in stocking (stockinette) stitch until work measures 31 (35:39)cm/12^1/$_4$ (13^3/$_4$:15^1/$_4$)in, ending with a purl row. ★★

SHAPE NECK: Row 1: cast off 10 (11:11) stitches, knit to end. **Row 2:** purl. **Row 3:** cast off 4 stitches, knit to end. Work 2 rows without shaping. Cast off.
With wrong side of work facing, rejoin yarn to remaining 62 (65:68) stitches at opening edge, knit 1 stitch, purl to end. Continue in stocking (stockinette) stitch until work measures 22 (25:28)cm/8^1/$_2$ (10:11)in, ending with a purl row.

SHAPE ARMHOLE: Row 1: cast off 2 stitches, knit to end. **Row 2:** knit 1 stitch, purl to end. **Row 3:** knit 2 stitches, knit 2 stitches together, knit to end. **Row 4:** knit 1 stitch, purl to end. Repeat rows 3 and 4 three times. *(56 (59:62) stitches)* Work from ★★ to ★★ as on first side but end with a knit row (work 1 row less).

SHAPE NECK: Row 1: cast of 10 (11:11) stitches, purl to end. **Row 2:** knit. **Row 3:** cast off 4 stitches, purl to end. Work 3 more rows without shaping. Cast off.

FRONT: Cast on and garter stitch border as for back. Change to stocking (stockinette) stitch and continue until work measures 22 (25:28)cm/8¹/₂ (10:11)in, ending with a purl row.

SHAPE ARMHOLE: Rows 1 and 2: cast off 2 stitches at the beginning of each row, work to end. **Row 3:** knit 2 stitches, knit 2 stitches together, knit to the last 4 stitches, knit 2 stitches together through the back loops, knit 2 stitches. **Row 4:** purl. Repeat rows 3 and 4 three times. *(113 (119:125) stitches)* **Decrease row:** ★ knit 2 stitches

above left: The sleeves are gently shaped by working simple decreases that give a fully-fashioned effect and trimmed with a simple rib stitch cuff.

above right: A picot edge is a simple yet pretty way to finish an otherwise plain neckline. It is an easy stitch yet very effective.

together 55 (58:61) times, knit 3 stitches together. *(56 (59:62) stitches)* Knit 3 rows to mark the front yoke. Continue in stocking (stockinette) stitch until work measures 29 (33:37)cm/11¹/₂ (13:14¹/₂)in, ending with a purl row.

SHAPE NECK: Next row: knit 21 (22:23) stitches, cast off 14 (15:16) stitches, knit 21 (22:23) stitches. Now work on the second set of 21 (22:23) stitches. ★★ Decrease 1 stitch at the neck on the next 7 rows. Work 4 rows. Cast off. ★★ With wrong side of work facing, rejoin yarn to the remaining 21 (22:23) stitches at the neck edge and work from ★★ to ★★ again.

SLEEVES: *Make 2 the same.* With 2.25mm (US 1) needles, cast on 47 (51:55) stitches and work 5 (7:7) rows in rib as follows: **Row 1:** ★ knit 1 stitch, purl 1 stitch, repeat from ★ to the last stitch, knit 1 stitch. **Row 2:** ★ purl 1 stitch, knit 1 stitch, repeat from ★ to the last stitch, purl 1 stitch. Repeat rows 1 and 2 once (twice:twice) more, then row 1 again.

Increase row: rib 1 (3:5) stitches, ★ up 1 stitch, rib 5 stitches, repeat from ★ to last 1 (3:5) stitches, up 1 stitch, rib 1 (3:5) stitches. *(57 (61 :65) stitches)* Change to 2.75mm (US 2) needles and work in stocking (stockinette) stitch. Increase 1 stitch at each end of the third row and every following alternate row until there are 67 (71:75) stitches. Work 3 more rows.

SHAPE SLEEVEHEAD: **Rows 1 and 2:** cast off 2 stitches at the beginning of each row; work to end. **Row 3:** knit 2 stitches, knit 2 stitches together, knit to the last 4 stitches, knit 2 stitches together through the back loops, knit 2 stitches. **Row 4:** purl. Repeat rows 3 and 4 three times. *(55 (59:63) stitches)* **Decrease row:** knit 2 (1:1) stitches ★ knit 2 stitches together, knit 4 stitches, repeat from ★ to last 5 (4:2) stitches, knit 2 stitches together, knit 3 (2:0) stitches. **Next row:** knit. Cast off.

NECKTRIM: Join shoulder seams. With right side of garment facing and using 2.75mm (US 2) needles, pick up and knit 14 (15:16) stitches from back opening to shoulder seam, 10 stitches down front neck, 14 (15:16) stitches from centre front neck, 10 stitches up front side neck and 14 (15:16) stitches from shoulder seam to back opening. *(62 (65:68) stitches)* Knit 1 row.

To work picot edge, cast off 3 stitches ★ slip the stitch on the right needle back on to the left needle, cast on 2 stitches, cast off 5 stitches. Repeat from ★ to the end of the row. Cast off the last stitch.

TO MAKE UP: Weave in all the loose ends. Lay work out flat and gently steam, ease in the sleeves between the armhole shaping, the straight edge of the sleeve fitting between the yokes, and the sloping edge attached to the body of the dress. Stitch into position. Join side and sleeve seams.

TO FINISH: Cut the length of ribbon in half and attach each piece securely to either side of the top of the back centre opening.

left: It is often difficult to get a wriggling baby in and out of its clothes. This dress has no fiddly buttons, the back being fastened simply with a ribbon tie, attached to either side of the back neck opening.

ribbon-tied wool vest

Another classic straight from the family photograph album, this little ribbon-edged vest is a brilliant gift for a new born baby. Knit it in classic white, or in soft blue, taupe or grey in merino or botany wool for extra winter warmth. Slot fine silk ribbon through the eyelets in the neck band, tied in a bow at the centre to create the finishing detail. The shoulder seams are grafted together for a smooth finish, ensuring that the baby's soft skin is not irritated.

how to make: ribbon-tied wool vest

above left: This design is best knitted in fine yarn, merino wool or cotton is the preferred choice for its natural qualities and ultimate comfort.

above centre: Simple eyelets are worked around the neck and threaded with fine silk (or possibly velvet) and tied in a bow. The fully fashioned detail at the neck edge gives an authentic touch to this classic garment.

SIZING: For sizing refer to chart on page 115.

MATERIALS: 2 (2:2) x 50g balls fine wool, e.g. Rowan true 4 ply botany yarn, Jaeger baby merino or Jaeger matchmaker 4 ply merino • Pair of 3mm (US 2) needles • Pair of 3.25mm (US 3) needles, plus spare • 6 safety pins • Sewing needle • Silk ribbon, 4mm (^{1}/$_4$in) wide and approximately 65cm (26 in) long

TENSION (GAUGE): 28 stitches and 36 rows to 10cm (4in) square measured over stocking (stockinette) stitch using 3.25mm (US 3) needles.

TECHNIQUES: Simple increases and decreases and bringing yarn forward to make an eyelet (see page 124).

METHOD: BACK: Using 3mm (US 2) needles, cast on 56 (62:68) stitches. Work 4 (4:6) rows in knit 1, purl 1 rib, every row: ★ knit 1 stitch, purl 1 stitch, repeat from ★ to end. Change to 3.25mm (US 3) needles and work in stocking (stockinette) stitch until the knitting measures 13.5 (15:16.5)cm/5^1/$_4$ (6:6^1/$_2$)in. Tie a coloured thread to each end of the next row to mark the armhole. Continue knitting until the work measures 16.5 (19:21.5)cm/6^1/$_2$ (7^1/$_2$:8^1/$_4$)in, ending with a purl row.

SHAPE NECK: Knit 22 (24:26) stitches, turn and work on these stitches as follows: ★ Decrease 1 stitch at the neck edge on every row until 14 (16:18) stitches remain.

above right: Simply shaped sleeves are set into the body. The shoulders are "grafted" together to give a flat appearance, with no bulky inside seams.

opposite: If you start in plenty of time for the baby's birth, you can knit several of these little vests and store them in a tiny linen basket to await the new arrival.

Continue until work measures 21.5 (24:26.5)cm/8^1/$_2$ (9^1/$_2$:10^1/$_2$)in. Break yarn and leave these stitches on a safety pin. ★ Slip the centre 12 (14:16) stitches onto a safety pin. With right side facing, rejoin the yarn to the remaining 22 (24:26) stitches at the neck edge and knit to the end of the row. Then work from ★ to ★ as on the first side.

FRONT: Work as for back.

SLEEVES: *Make 2 the same.* Using 3mm (US 2) needles, cast on 46 (50:54) stitches and work 4 rows in knit 1, purl 1 rib as on back.
Change to 3.25mm (US 3) needles and work in stocking (stockinette) stitch for 2 (2.5:3)cm/^{3}/$_4$ (1:1^1/$_4$)in.

SHAPE SLEEVEHEAD: Decrease 1 stitch at the beginning of the next 10 rows. Cast off.

TO MAKE UP: Place 14 (16:18) right shoulder stitches onto 3.25mm (US 3) needles.

GRAFT SHOULDER SEAM: Hold the two needles with equal number of shoulder stitches on together, with the fabric wrong sides of the knitting facing each other, in the left hand. Using a spare needle, place the point of the right needle through the first stitch of the front and the back needle and knit together, do the same to the next two stitches on the left needles, and then cast off by pulling second stitch on right needle over first stitch on right needle. Continue like this along the row until all the stitches have been cast off. This will form a detail ridge row on the right side of the fabric.

NECKTRIM: Using 3mm (US 2) needles and with the right side of the work facing you, pick up and knit 14 (15:16) stitches along the left front side neck, 12 (14:16) stitches from the safety pin, 14 (15:16) stitches along the right front side neck to the shoulder, 14 (15:16) stitches down back right side neck, 12 (14:16) stitches from the safety pin and finally 14 (15:16) stitches from along the left back side neck. *(80 (88:96) stitches)* **Row 1:** purl 1 stitch, knit 1 stitch, alternately to the end of the row.

MAKE EYELETS: **Row 2:** ★ purl 1 stitch, knit 1 stitch, yarn forward, knit 2 stitches together, repeat from ★ to the end. **Row 3:** purl 1 stitch, knit 1 stitch alternately to the end of the row. **Row 4:** cast off in rib as set.

TO FINISH: Graft the other shoulder seam. Weave in all ends along the work, not up the sides. Lay work out flat and gently steam. Set sleeveheads between the coloured threads and stitch. Join side and sleeve seams. Join necktrim at shoulder. Thread the ribbon through the eyelets and tie at centre front.

opposite: This vintage-style vest, knitted in soft fine merino wool or light cool cotton, cossets the baby as the natural fibres allow the body to breathe, while keeping the baby comfortable.

rosebud cardigan

An ideal gift for a special occasion, this pretty stocking (stockinette) stitch cardigan is knitted in silk or mercerized cotton. The pearly sheen of the yarn is emphasized with a delicate rosebud trim or mother-of-pearl buttons. The front neck band is knitted integrally, giving it a very neat finish. Knit it up in bronze or grey for a small boy, without the rosebud trim. The decreasing stitches on the raglan shoulders are knitted two stitches in from the edge to create an attractive fully fashioned detail and a neater edge for sewing up.

how to make: **rosebud cardigan**

opposite: This timeless little cardigan, made in silk and trimmed with rosebuds or natural mother-of-pearl ensures its value as a new hand-me-down or heirloom piece.

SIZING: For sizing refer to chart on page 115.

MATERIALS: 2 (2:3) x 50g balls of fine yarn, e.g. Jaeger 4 ply silk or Jaeger 4 ply Siena cotton • Pair of 2.75mm (US 2) needles • Pair of 2.25mm • (US 1) needles • Sewing needle • 4 rosebuds or buttons

TENSION (GAUGE): 30 stitches and 38 rows to 10cm (4in) square measured over stocking (stockinette) stitch using 2.75mm (US 2) needles.

TECHNIQUES: Work the cast on edge with a size smaller needle to neaten the edge. For this pattern, you also need to be able to work increases and decreases, make eyelets, knit through the back of the loops and pick up stitches (see page 124 for explanations).

METHOD: BACK: Using 2.75mm (US 2) needles cast on 68 (76:84) stitches and work 6 rows in garter stitch, every row knit. Change to stocking (stockinette) stitch and work 34 (40:48) rows.

SHAPE RAGLAN ARMHOLE: Cast off 3 (3:2) stitches at the beginning of the next two rows. Work fully fashioned detail as follows: **Row 1:** knit 1 stitch, knit next 2 stitches together, knit to last 3 stitches, knit next 2 stitches together through the back loops, knit the last stitch. **Row 2:** purl. Repeat rows 1 and 2 until 28 (30:32) stitches remain. Cast off.

LEFT FRONT: Using 2.75mm (US 2) needles, cast on 36 (40:44) stitches and work 6 rows in garter stitch, every row knit. Change to stocking (stockinette) stitch with garter stitch button band as follows: **Row 1:** knit.

Row 2: knit 4 stitches, purl to end. Repeat rows 1 and 2 16 (19:23) times. *(34 (40:48) rows)*

SHAPE RAGLAN ARMHOLE: Row 1: cast off 3 (3:2) stitches, knit to end. **Row 2:** knit 4 stitches, purl to end. **Row 3:** knit 1 stitch, knit 2 stitches together, knit to end. **Row 4:** knit 4 stitches, purl to end. Repeat rows 3 and 4 until 21 (22:23) stitches remain, ending with row 3.

SHAPE NECK: Cast off 7 (8:9) stitches, purl to end. Now decrease 1 stitch at each end of every row until 2 stitches remain. Knit 2 stitches together. Fasten off.

RIGHT FRONT: Using 2.75mm (US 2) needles, cast on 36 (40:44) stitches and work 6 rows in garter stitch. Change to stocking (stockinette) stitch with garter stitch buttonhole band as follows: **Row 1:** knit across row. **Row 2:** purl to last 4 stitches, knit 4 stitches.

WORK THE FIRST BUTTONHOLE: Row 3: knit 2 stitches, yarn forward, knit 2 stitches together, knit to the end. Work 32 (38:46) more rows *(35 (41:49) rows)*, making second buttonhole (as row 3) on row 23 (27:33).

SHAPE RAGLAN ARMHOLE: (WRONG SIDE FACING): Row 1: cast off 3 (3:2) stitches, purl to last 4 stitches, knit 4 stitches. **Row 2:** knit to last 3 stitches, knit next 2 stitches together through the back loops, knit 1 stitch. **Row 3:** purl to last 4 stitches, knit 4 stitches. Repeat rows 2 and 3 until 28 (31:35) stitches remain, ending with row 3. **Next row:** make buttonhole: knit 2 stitches, yarn forward, knit 2 stitches together, knit to last 3 stitches, knit next 2 stitches through the back loops, knit 1 stitch. Continue raglan shaping until 22 (23:24) stitches remain, ending with a purl row.

SHAPE NECK: Cast off 7 (8:9) stitches, knit to last 3 stitches, knit next 2 stitches together through the back loops, knit 1 stitch. **Next row:** purl across row. Decrease 1 stitch at each end of every row until 2 stitches remain. Knit 2 stitches together. Fasten off.

LEFT SLEEVE: Using 2.75mm (US 2) needles cast on 36 (42:48) stitches and work 6 rows in garter stitch, every row knit. Change to stocking (stockinette) stitch. Increase each end of first and every following 4th row to 52 (60:68) stitches. Continue without shaping until work measures 10 (13:16)cm/4 (5:6)in, ending with a purl row.

SHAPE RAGLAN ARMHOLE: Cast off 3 (3:2) stitches at the beginning of the next 2 rows. Decrease 1 stitch,

above left: The garter stitch button and buttonhole bands are knitted at the same time as the fronts, this gives a much neater appearance and less sewing up! Decorative rosebuds are used in place of conventional buttons.

above right: Work the decrease stitches for the raglan shaping 2 stitches in from the edge to give a fully-fashioned detail and a neater edge for sewing up.

fully fashioned, as on back, at each end of the next and every following alternate row until 22 (24:26) stitches remain,

ending with a purl row. Now decrease 1 stitch at each end of every row until 8 (10:12) stitches remain, ending with a knit row. Cast off 3 (4:5) stitches, purl to the last 3 stitches, purl 2 stitches together, purl 1 stitch.

Next row: knit 1 stitch, knit 2 stitches together, knit to end. Cast off.

RIGHT SLEEVE: Work as for the left sleeve until 10 (12:14) stitches remain, ending with a purl row. Cast off 3 (4:5) stitches, knit to the last 3 stitches, knit 2 stitches together through the back of loops, knit 1 stitch. **Next row:** Purl 1 stitch, purl 2 stitches together through the back loops, purl 1 (2:3) stitches, purl 2 stitches together. Cast off.

TO MAKE UP: Weave in all ends. Lay work flat, pin down if necessary. Gently steam. Sew front and back raglan seams, with the highest point of sleeve, towards the back. Sew the sleeve and side seams.

NECKBAND: With 2.75mm (US 2) needles and with the right side of the work facing you, pick up and knit 13 (14:15) stitches from right front neck, 6 (7:8) stitches across top of right sleeve, 28 (30:32) stitches across the back neck, 6 (7:8) stitches across top of left sleeve, 13 (14:15) stitches from left front neck. *(66 (72:78) stitches)* Work 3 rows in garter stitch, making a buttonhole on the first row, as follows: knit to last 4 stitches, knit 2 stitches together, yarn forward, knit 2 stitches. Change to 2.75mm (US 1) needles and knit 1 more row. Cast off.

TO FINISH: Sew up the side and sleeve seams. Attach rosebuds or buttons of your choice to match the buttonholes.

above: A simple raglan sleeve, round-neck style updated in luxurious silk creates a traditional baby cardigan with a twist. Silk takes colour beautifully, so you will be tempted to knit this design over and over again in different colours as gifts for the new arrivals of friends and family.

simple lavender bag

One of the best soporofic herbs, lavender is the ideal stuffing for a simple bag to tuck under the baby's pillow or to hang from the closet door, to scent the baby's room. Knitted in one piece in stocking (stockinette) stitch, with a fine picot edge at the opening, the bag is tied with fine silk ribbon. If you are giving the lavender bag as a present, tie a small silver charm to the ribbon.

how to make: **simple lavender bag**

SIZE: This bag measures 12 x 16cm (4³/₄ x 6¹/₄in)

MATERIALS: 1 x 50g ball of fine silk yarn, e.g. Jaeger 4 ply silk • Pair of 2mm (US 1) needles • Sewing needle • Fine ribbon to trim • Thin muslin, silk or fine cotton fabric for sachet

TENSION (GAUGE): 36 stitches and 46 rows to 10m (4in) square measured over stocking (stockinette) stitch using 2mm (US 1) needles.

TECHNIQUES: Bringing yarn forward to make an eyelet through which ribbon is threaded (see page 124 for explanation).

METHOD: Using 2mm (US 1) needles, cast on 83 stitches and work 12cm (4³/₄in) in stocking (stockinette) stitch, ending with a purl row.

MAKE EYELETS: Knit 5 stitches, ★ yarn forward, knit 2 stitches together, knit 8 stitches, repeat from ★, ending last repeat, knit 6 stitches. Work for another 3cm (1¹/₄in)

above left: Fold the finished knitting in half widthways; with the picot edge at the top, and sew along the side and bottom edges.

above centre: A little sachet, filled with lavender seed-heads, is inserted into the finished knitted bag.

above right: Thread fine silk ribbon through the eyelets at the top of the knitted bag, draw it up and fasten it with a decorative bow.

opposite: Lavender has long been recognized as conducive to restful sleep, so place it in the baby's bedding or put it under your own pillow!

in stocking (stockinette) stitch, ending with a purl row.

PICOT EDGE: Cast off 3 stitches, ★ slip the stitch on the right needle back on to the left needle, cast on 2 stitches, cast off 5 stitches. Repeat from ★ to the end of the row. Cast off the last stitch.

TO MAKE UP: Lay the knitting out flat and gently steam. With the right sides of the knitting together, fold the work in half widthways, with the picot edge at the top. Sew along the side and bottom edge. Thread ribbon through the eyelets.

LAVENDER SACHET: Cut a rectangle of fabric 12cm (4³/₄in) wide and 26cm (10¹/₄in) deep. Fold in half lengthwise and sew the two side seams, leaving the top open. Fill bag with lavender seeds. Turn the top edge over and sew up securely.

TO FINISH: Put lavender, sachet into knitted bag. Pull up ribbon and tie in a decorative bow at the front.

finishing touches

above left: When you fold the garments or knitted projects, insert tissue paper between the layers to prevent creasing.

above centre: Metallic paper, finished with gauze ribbon, makes a neat package for a small present.

above right: For a modern touch, wrap up the gift in brown paper, tie it with string and add a small present, like this wooden rattle, with the gift tag.

opposite: Knitted gifts on their way to a baby shower.

IF YOU GO to the trouble of knitting for a new baby, then make sure that you finish off your knitted gift appropriately. Take time and care with the finishing details. All too often the final touches to a beautifully knitted garment are rushed in the euphoria of completing the project. By taking time with the detail of putting the pieces together a professional finish will be achieved. Weave in all the ends along the row at the back of the knitting, never up the side, as this will give bulky seams. Lay the pieces out flat on the wrong or reverse side and press the knitting with a steam iron or press gently under a damp cloth. Do not flatten the knitting or stretch it out of shape. When you have to join up sections of knitting, make sure you join each piece in turn, matching rows, and taking time to line up pieces accurately. Sewing stitches used in joining up should be neat and unobtrusive. (For further information on techniques, see page 124.) Any trims or embellishments should be chosen with care to match both the colour and style of the garment and need to be securely attached to it.

giftwrapping ideas

Many of us are induced to knit for a baby when a close friend or relative becomes pregnant. If you want to offer something you have knitted to a friend or relative as a gift to welcome the newborn baby, do take care to present it beautifully. It becomes a token of your love and esteem, and will be very much appreciated. Nothing is too good for the new baby!

The best way to wrap any kind of present is with simplicity and style. Make sure that the knitted garment or project is neatly folded, ideally layered with tissue paper to prevent it creasing. Choose plain good-quality paper for wrapping, and find novel forms of tie, rather than the ubiquitous cheap ribbon. If you wrap the gift carefully, you can avoid the use of sticky tape, and the paper is then reusable. String, raffia or unusual ribbons can be used instead to package the parcel. Why not add a small additional present, in the shape of a baby's rattle or a small charm, as a finishing detail, tied to the ribbon? And don't forget to add a matching tag with a special message of congratulations. You can make these yourself very easily from pieces of card.

helpful information

care of yarns

A BABY'S SKIN IS SOFT, delicate and very sensitive, and great care should be taken in the laundering of their clothes. One thing is certain; baby clothes will require frequent washing. The yarn you use must be able to stand up to this frequent washing, but this does not necessarily mean that all yarns must be machine washable.

Look at the labels: those on most commercial yarns have instructions for washing or dry cleaning, drying and pressing. So for a project knitted in one yarn only, a quick look at the yarn label will tell you how to care for it. If you wish to work with several yarns in one piece of work, the aftercare requires a little more thought. If one label suggests dry cleaning, then be sure to dry clean the garment.

If in doubt about whether your knitting is washable, then make a little swatch of the yarns. Wash this to see if the fabric is affected by being immersed in water or not, watching out for shrinkage and stretching. If you are satisfied with the results, go ahead and wash the knitting by hand in lukewarm water. Never use hot water, as this will "felt" your fabric, and you will not be able to return it to its pre-washed state. Take care, too, to keep the rinsing water the same temperature as the washing water. Wool, in particular, tends to react to major changes in temperature.

Natural fibres such as wool, cotton and silk are usually better washed by hand, and in pure soap, than in a machine. Soap flakes are kinder to baby's skin than that of most detergents, provided all traces of the soap are removed in the rinsing process.

Washing: When washing the finished knitting, handle it carefully. There should be enough water to cover the garment completely and the soap should be thoroughly dissolved before immersing it. If you need to sterilize any garment that has become badly soiled or stained, then use a proprietary brand of sterilizer for this purpose.

Rinsing: Squeeze out excess water, never wring it out. Rinse thoroughly, until every trace of soap is removed, as any left in will matt the fibres and may irritate the baby's skin. Use at least two changes of water or continue until the water is clear and without bubbles.

Spinning: The garments can be rinsed on a short rinse and spin as part of a normal washing machine programme for delicate fabrics.

As a precaution, test wash any ribbons or trims you use before you make up the garment with them. Nothing is more infuriating than to spoil an entire garment because the trim colours run in the wash!

Drying: Squeeze the garment between towels or fold in a towel and gently spin.

Do not hang wet knitting up, as the weight of the water will stretch it out of shape. To dry, lay the knitting out flat on top of a towel, or an old terry nappy (diaper) which will absorb some of the moisture. Ease the garment into shape. Dry away from direct heat and leave flat until completely dry.

Pressing: When the garment is dry, ease it into shape. Check the yarn label before pressing your knitting as most fibres only require a little steam, and the iron should be applied gently. Alternatively, press with a damp cloth between the garment and the iron.

Removing stains: Stains are a fact of life in bringing up a baby. Most of the stains that are likely to affect a baby's clothing are to do with foods. The best solution with any stain is to remove the garment while the stain is still wet and soak it thoroughly in cold, not hot, water. Failing that use a proprietary stain remover.

opposite: Natural fibres such as wool, cotton and silk are usually better washed by hand. Wash the finished knitting carefully and rinse thoroughly, before drying it flat on a rack.

sizing tables

INSTRUCTIONS ARE given in three sizes for each project; the figures for the larger sizes are given inside brackets. Sizes are given by age and weight but are intended as an average guide only. More detailed measurements for body length, body width and sleeve length for each project are given in the following tables.

above: The pattern for the classic cashmere sweater can be found on page 20 and the pattern for the matching leggings on page 26.

right: The pattern for the classic cashmere bootees can be found on page 32.

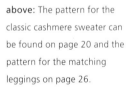

classic cashmere sweater

TO FIT SIZES	1	2	3
BABY AGED (MONTHS)	0–3	3–6	6–9
FINISHED CHEST CM (IN)	48 (19)	55 (21^1/$_2$)	62 (24^1/$_2$)
BACK LENGTH CM (IN)	21.5 (8^1/$_2$)	25 (10)	29 (11^1/$_2$)

classic cashmere leggings

TO FIT SIZES	1	2	3
BABY AGED (MONTHS)	0–3	3–6	6–9
HIP CM (IN)	53 (21)	57 (22^1/$_2$)	60 (23^1/$_2$)
INSIDE LEG CM (IN)	24 (9^1/$_2$)	27 (10^1/$_2$)	29 (11^1/$_2$)

classic cashmere bootees

TO FIT SIZES	1	2	3
BABY AGED (MONTHS)	0–3	3–6	6–9
FOOT LENGTH CM (IN)	9 (3^1/$_2$)	10.5 (4^1/$_8$)	12 (4^3/$_4$)

right: The pattern for the garter stitch cardigan can be found on page 36.

centre: The pattern for the chunky knit cardigan can be found on page 50.

below: The pattern for the baby's beanie hat can be found on page 54

garter stitch cardigan

TO FIT SIZES	1	2	3
BABY AGED (MONTHS)	0–3	3–6	6–9
FINISHED CHEST CM (IN)	46 (18)	52 (20^1/$_2$)	58 (23)
BACK LENGTH CM (IN)	21 (8^1/$_4$)	23 (9)	25 (9^1/$_4$)
SLEEVE LENGTH FROM CENTRE BACK CM (IN)	20 (8)	23 (9)	25 (10)

chunky knit cardigan

TO FIT SIZES	1	2	3
BABY AGED (MONTHS)	0–3	3–6	6–9
FINISHED CHEST CM (IN)	46 (18)	52 (20^1/$_2$)	58 (23)
BACK LENGTH CM (IN)	19 (7^1/$_2$)	21 (8^1/$_2$)	23 (9)
SLEEVE LENGTH FROM CENTRE BACK CM (IN)	28 (11)	30 (11^3/$_4$)	32 (12^1/$_2$)

baby's beanie hat

TO FIT SIZES	1	2	3
BABY AGED (MONTHS)	0–3	3–6	6–9
HEAD CIRCUMFERENCE CM (IN)	34 (13^1/$_2$)	38 (15)	42 (16^1/$_2$)

right: The pattern for the garter stitch wrap top can be found on page 58.

centre: The pattern for the vintage cardigan can be found on page 66.

below: The pattern for the garter stitch silk slippers can be found on page 80.

garter stitch wrap top

TO FIT SIZES	1	2	3
BABY AGED (MONTHS)	0–3	3–6	6–9
FINISHED CHEST CM (IN)	35.5 (14)	40.5 (16)	46 (18)
BACK LENGTH CM (IN)	16.5 (6$^1/_2$)	19 (7$^1/_2$)	21.5 (8$^1/_2$)

vintage cardigan

TO FIT SIZES	1	2	3
BABY AGED (MONTHS)	0–3	3–6	6–9
FINISHED CHEST CM (IN)	48 (19)	53 (21)	58 (23)
BACK LENGTH CM (IN)	20 (8)	23 (9)	25.5 (10)
SLEEVE SEAM CM (IN)	14 (5$^1/_2$)	17 (6$^1/_2$)	19 (7$^1/_2$)

garter stitch silk slippers

TO FIT SIZES	1	2	3
BABY AGED (MONTHS)	0–3	3–6	6–9
FINISH FOOT LENGTH CM (IN)	9 (3$^1/_2$)	10 (4)	11 (4$^1/_4$)

right: The pattern for the traditional mabel dress can be found on page 84.

centre: The pattern for the ribbon-tied wool vest can be found on page 90.

below: The pattern for the rosebud cardigan can be found on page 96.

traditional mabel dress

TO FIT SIZES	1	2	3
BABY AGED (MONTHS)	0–3	3–6	6–9
LENGTH CM (IN)	30 (12)	33 (3)	11 (14^1/$_4$)
FINISHED CHEST (AROUND YOKE)	43 (17)	46 (18)	48.5 (19)

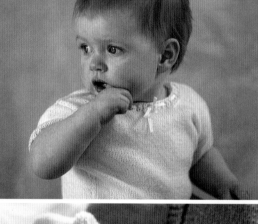

ribbon-tied wool vest

TO FIT SIZES	1	2	3
BABY AGED (MONTHS)	0–3	3–6	6–9
FINISHED CHEST CM (IN)	37 (14^1/$_2$)	42 (16^1/$_2$)	47 (18^1/$_2$)
LENGTH FROM SHOULDER CM (IN)	21.5 (8^1/$_2$)	24 (9^1/$_2$)	26.5 (10^1/$_2$)

rosebud cardigan

TO FIT SIZES	1	2	3
BABY AGED (MONTHS)	0–3	3–6	6–9
ACTUAL CHEST CM (IN)	46 (18)	51 (20)	56 (22)
BACK LENGTH CM (IN)	18 (7)	22 (8^1/$_2$)	26 (10)
SLEEVE LENGTH FROM CENTRE BACK CM (IN)	10 (4)	13 (5)	15 (6)

charts

SOME PATTERNS IN THIS BOOK require charts. Each square on the charts shown here represents a stitch and each horizontal line of squares on each chart represents a row of knitting.

When reading from the charts read odd-numbered rows as knit rows (from right to left) and read even-numbered rows as purl rows (from left to right).

For ease in reading charts it may be helpful to have the chart enlarged at a printers and then make any markings, such as row numbers, or notes that you may require as you work.

An alphabet is depicted here for working the baby blanket and baby cushion but you can use it for working alternative names or messages to personalize your projects. Each letter block is 24 stitches wide and 30 rows high, and is knitted in reverse stocking (stockinette) stitch, i.e. purl on the knit rows and knit on the purl rows. To work the letters start reading at the bottom right hand corner marked by see B, D and F, or the edge of the letter, see A, C and E.

Similarly charts are given for the cashmere teddy bear (page 123), should you find it easier to work from a chart than follow the written instructions. The sssh! baby sleeping chart (page 123) is for counted cross stitch embroidery, the centre being on the bottom row of bébé between é and b above the X.

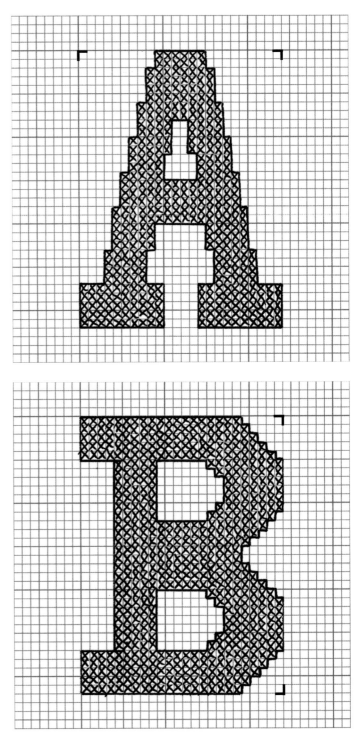

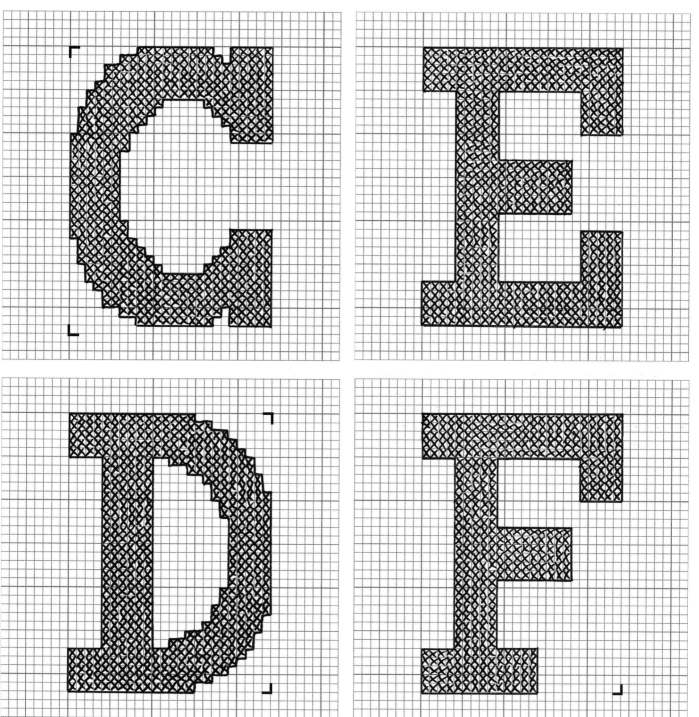

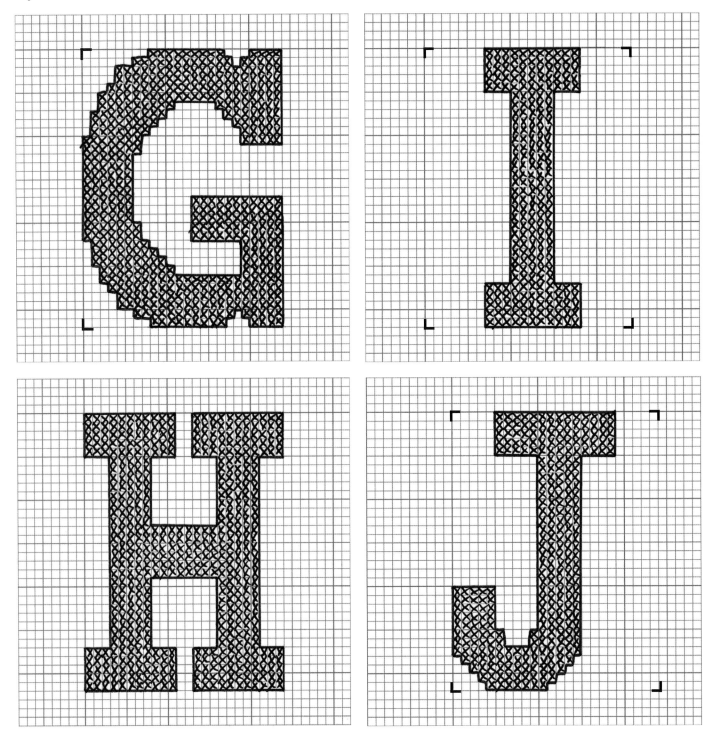

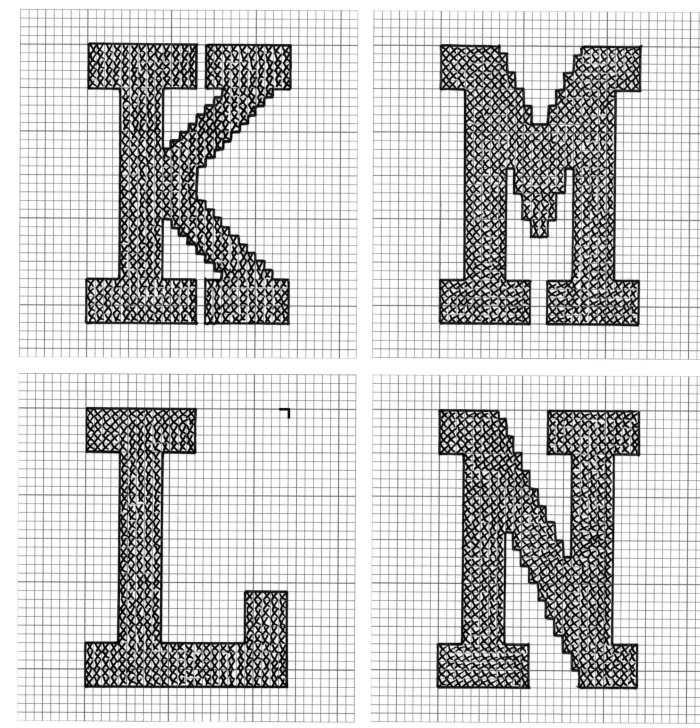

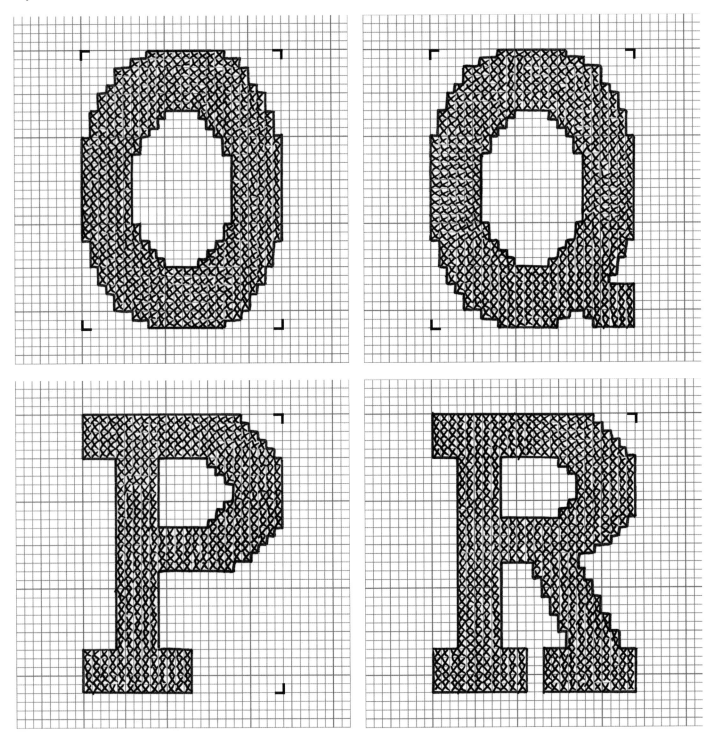

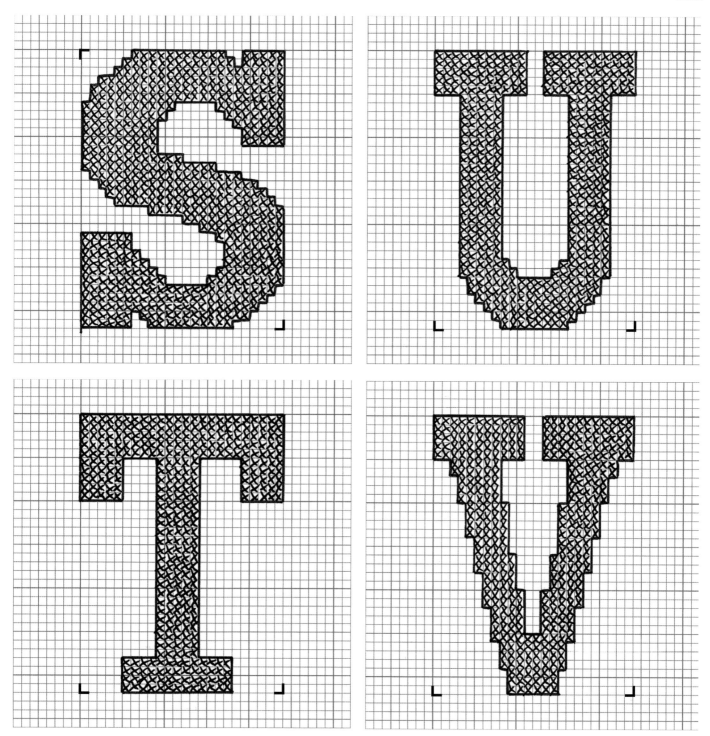

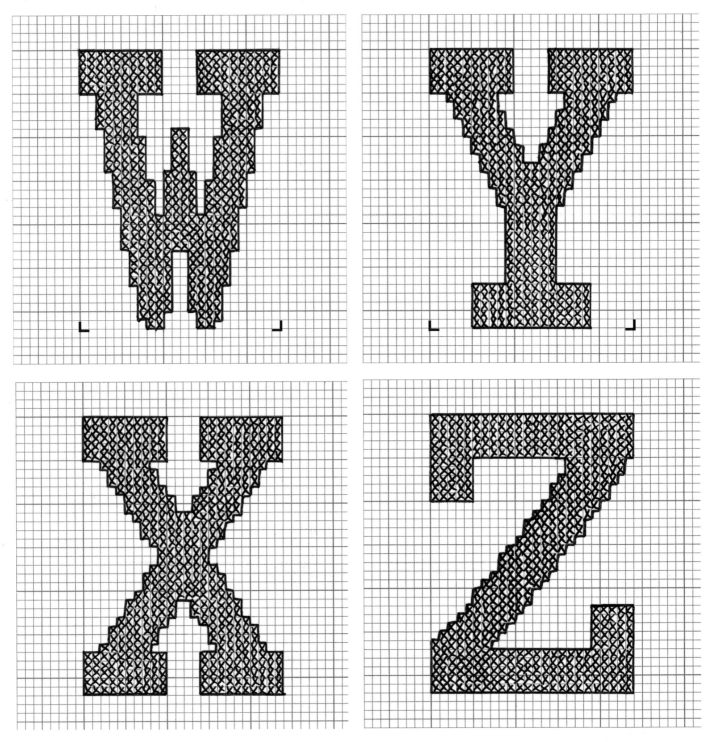

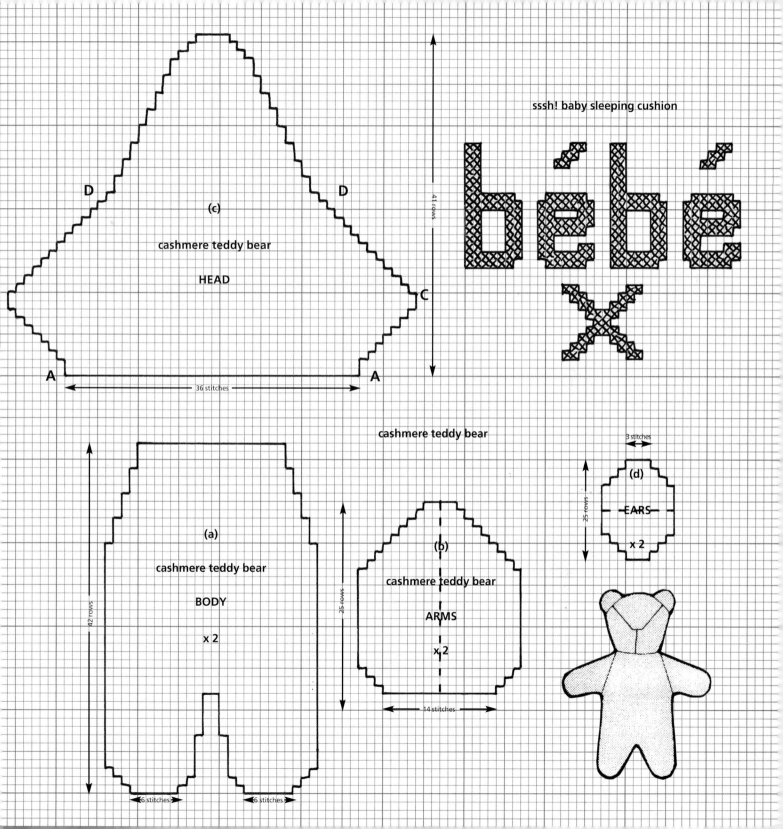

sssh! baby sleeping cushion

D (c) D

cashmere teddy bear

HEAD

C

A ← 36 stitches → A

41 rows

cashmere teddy bear

(a)

cashmere teddy bear

BODY

x 2

42 rows

6 stitches   6 stitches

(b)

cashmere teddy bear

ARMS

x 2

25 rows

14 stitches

3 stitches

(d)

EARS

x 2

25 rows

technique **glossary**

A FEW SPECIAL TECHNIQUES are used throughout the patterns in this book. For those who are unfamiliar with them, a brief explanation follows.

KNITTING TECHNIQUES:

Slip the first stitch
Transfer the stitch from the left needle to the right needle without knitting it.

Through the back loops
Put the right needle through the back loops of the next 2 stitches and knit or purl them together as though they were 1 stitch. On a purl row this takes a little practice.

Increase
Knit or purl the next stitch but do not drop it off the needle. Slip the point of the right needle through the back of the stitch and knit another stitch in the usual way, then drop the stitch from the left needle. You have made 2 stitches out of 1 stitch.

Decrease
Knit or purl the next 2 stitches together. You have made 1 stitch out of 2 stitches.

Yarn forward
Used to make a 'hole'. Bring yarn forward as if to purl, take it back over the right needle, then work the next instruction.

Yarn over
Used to make a 'hole'. Take yarn over right needle, from front to back of work and then under the right needle to the front of work, then work the next instruction.

Pick up stitches
Insert the right needle through the stitch or short loop along the edge of the piece of knitting to be attached and knit a stitch in the usual way. Do this, evenly spaced, for the required number of stitches.

Up 1 stitch
Make a stitch without leaving a hole by putting the right needle under the horizontal thread before the next stitch and placing this thread onto the left needle to make a stitch. Knit it through the back loop.

Chart reading
Each small square represents a stitch and a row. Read the knit rows from right to left and the purl rows from left to right.

SEWING TECHNIQUES:

Invisible seaming
Work with right sides facing, a blunt needle and the same yarn as the work. Place both pieces to be joined side by side, edges butted up and beginning at the lower edge, insert the needle down through the centre of a knitted stitch and then back up through centre of the stitch next to it. Repeat this action in the edge of the adjoining piece. Returning to the first piece, insert the needle down through the stitch it came out of, then back up through centre of next stitch to it. Repeat this zigzag action for the length of the entire seam, gently pulling the seam into shape as you work.

Mattress stitch
This is another name for invisible seaming (see instructions above).

yarn buying **information**

THE SECRET TO GETTING the most out of a yarn is to experiment with it, trying out various needles sizes and seeing how it works in different stitch patterns.

I have recommended or suggested a yarn type for each project, which is of good quality and specifically suited to baby garments.

If you cannot find the particular yarn specified or suggested in the instructions, any other make of yarn that is of the same weight and type should serve as well, but, to avoid disappointing results, it is very important that you work a tension swatch first that matches that given in each project, changing the needle size if necessary to achieve the correct tension.

Substituting yarns: I make every effort to use yarns and colours that are in spinners ranges at time of going to press, however, spinners reserve the right to discontinue their yarns due to seasonal strategy. So wherever possible, I do try to be generic both with yarn and colour. As some yarns or colours may no longer be available I have listed possible alternatives that you may wish to consider.

If you decide to use an alternative yarn, in order to find a specific shade or because you cannot obtain the yarn recommended, be sure to purchase a substitute yarn that is as close as possible to the original in thickness, weight and texture so that it will be compatible with the knitting instructions.

Buy one ball only to start with, so you can test the effect and the tension. Calculate quantities required using information about lengths, yardage or meterage found on the ball bands.

Actual yarns used: The following is a list of the yarns used for the projects in the book and some suggested alternatives for substitution. The yarn characteristics given will be helpful when trying to find an alternative yarn.

FINE YARNS:

Jaeger silk 4 ply: a 4 ply silk yarn (100 per cent pure silk), approximately 186m (201yd) per 50g ball.
Recommended tension is 28 stitches and 38 rows to 10cm (4in) using 3mm (US 2) needles.

Jaeger matchmaker merino 4 ply: a 4 ply wool yarn (100 per cent merino wool), approximately 183m (200yd) per 50g ball.
Recommended tension is 28 stitches and 36 rows to 10cm (4in) using 3.25mm (US 3) needles.

Jaeger Siena 4 ply: a 4 ply mercerized cotton yarn (100 per cent pure cotton), approximately 140m (153yd) per 50g ball.
Recommended tension is 28 stitches and 38 rows to 10cm (4in) using 2.75–3mm [US 2–3] needles.

Rowan true 4 ply botany: a 4 ply wool yarn (100 per cent pure new wool), approximately 170m (185yd) per 50g ball.
Recommended tension is 28 stitches and 36 rows to 10cm (4in) using 3.25mm (US 3) needles.

FINE YARN SUBSTITUTIONS:

*Rowan Classic cashsoft 4 ply: a 4 ply wool yarn; 57 per cent extra fine merino/33 per cent microfibre/10 per cent cashmere. Approx 180m (197yd) per 50g ball.
Recommended tension is 28 stitches and 36 rows to 10cm (4in) using 3.25mm (US 3) needles.

Rowan 4 ply soft: a 4 ply wool yarn; 100 per cent merino wool. Approx 175m (191yd) per 50g ball.
Recommended tension is 28 stitches and 36 rows to 10cm (4in) using 3.25mm (US 3) needles.

Rowan Classic Siena 4 ply: a 4 ply mercerized cotton yarn 100 per cent pure cotton. Approx 140m (153yd) per 50g ball.
Recommended tension is 28 stitches and 38 rows to 10cm (4in) using 3mm (US 2) needles.

Rowan purewool 4 ply: a 4 ply wool yarn; 100 per cent pure wool. Approx 160m (191yd) per 50g ball.
Recommended tension is 28 stitches and 36 rows to 10cm (4in) using 3.25mm (US 3) needles.

MEDIUM YARNS:

Jaeger cashmere: a 4 ply yarn, but knits as a double knitting weight yarn (90 per cent cashmere/10 per cent polyamide), approximately 98m (107yd) per 50g ball.
Recommended tension is 28 stitches and 36 rows to 10cm (4in) using 3.25mm (US 3) needles.

Jaeger aqua cotton DK: a double knitting weight cotton yarn (100 per cent mercerized cotton), approximately 106m (115yd) per 50g ball.
Recommended tension is 22 stitches and 30 rows to 10cm (4in) using 4mm (US 6) needles.

Rowan wool/cotton: a double knitting weight blend yarn (50 per cent merino wool, 50 per cent cotton), approximately 113m (123yd) per 50g ball.
Recommended tension is 22–24 stitches and 30–32 rows to 10cm (4in) using 3.25–4 mm (US 5–6) needles.

MEDIUM YARN SUBSTITUTIONS:

* Rowan cotton glace: a light double knitting weight cotton yarn; 100 per cent cotton. Approx 115m (126yd) per 50g ball.
Recommended tension is 23 stitches and 32 rows to 10 cm (4in) using 3.25–3.75mm (US 3–5) needles.

Rowan Classic Baby Alpaca DK: a double knitting weight yarn; 100 per cent baby alpaca. Approx 100m (109yd) per 50g ball.
Recommended tension is 22 stitches and 30 rows to 10cm (4in) using 4mm (US 6) needles.
Work on a smaller needle if making cashmere teddy bear on page 62.]

Rowan Purelife organic cotton naturally dyed: a double knitting weight blend yarn; 100 per cent certified organic cotton. Approx 120m (131yd) per 50g ball.
Recommended tension is 22 stitches and 30 rows to 10 cm (4in) [using 3.75mm (US 5) needles.

CHUNKY YARNS:

Rowan all seasons cotton: An Aran or chunky weight yarn (60 per cent cotton/40 per cent acrylic), approximately 90m (98yd) per 50g ball.
Recommended tension is 16–18 stitches and 23–25 rows to 10cm(4in) using 4.5–5.5mm(US 7–9) needles.

suppliers

See previous pages for information about the Rowan yarns used in this book. Rowan yarns are widely distributed. To find the most up-to-date list of distributors and stores in your area, contact Rowan in the UK or Westminster Fibers in the US.

Rowan
Green Lane Mill
Holmfirth
West Yorkshire
HD9 2DX
England
Telephone: +44 (0) 1484 681 881
www.knitrowan.com

Westminster Fibers, Inc.
165 Ledge Street
Nashua
NH 03060
USA
Telephone: +1 (603) 886-5041
www.westminsterfibers.com

acknowledgements

This book is dedicated to the anonymous women who have knitted, stitched and created for their children, their children's children, and the children of their families and friends of successive generations. I have sought and bought their work from flea markets and charity shops the world over. Their love and care has been crafted into every fibre and stitch. Many of these women have had no formal training, just a passion for their craft, taught and passed down to them over the generations. They are my inspiration.

My sincerest thanks to the many people who have contributed to the creation of this book. They are a very special team, selected for their professionalism, enthusiasm, creativity, dedication, patience, attention to detail and endless support. I would like to thank, in particular, Susan Berry, John Heseltine, Debbie Mole, Eva Yates, Claire Waite Brown, Sally Lee and Sarah Phillips. I would also like to thank Kate Kirby, Clare Lattin and Niamh Hatton at Collins & Brown, Shephen Sheard and the Rowan Yarns and Jaeger teams, Rosalynn Kennedy, Ian and Bella Harris and the mothers and babies who so kindly agreed to be photographed for this book, along with the teddy bear, kindly loaned by Debbie Mole. I would like to thank Claudia for the original inspiration.

Love crafts?

We are all crazy about crafts in **C&B**, be it knitting, crochet, dress-making or embroidery, our offices are crammed with samples, patterns and new ideas. We hope our books reflect our enthusiasm!

To keep up to date with our latest books, author events across the country and competitions, please visit **www.collinsandbrown.co.uk**

Join our newsletter! Our crafts editor will send you the latest from C&B HQ each month. Just email: **lovecrafts@anovabooks.com**

"We'd love to hear from you!
At C&B, we make the craft world a better place."

Collins & Brown, an imprint of Anova Books
www.anovabooks.com

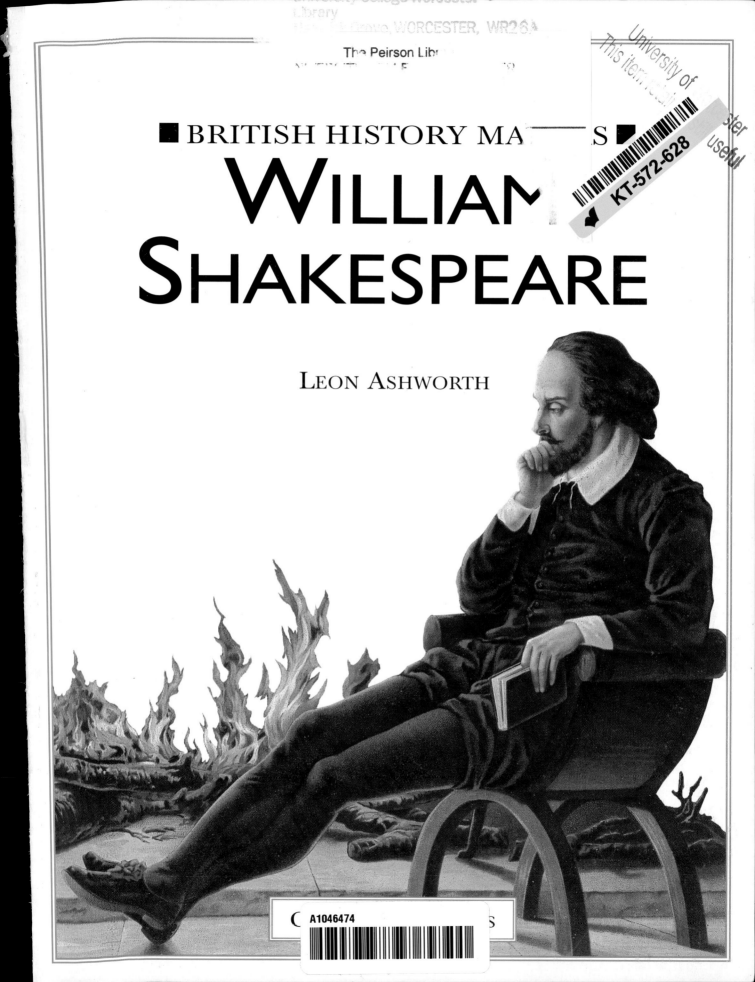

BRITISH HISTORY MAKERS

WILLIAM SHAKESPEARE

Leon Ashworth

A Cherrytree Book

Designed and produced by
A S Publishing

Copyright © this edition
Evans Brothers Ltd 2005

Published in 2005
by Cherrytree Press,
a division of Evans Brothers Ltd
2A Portman Mansions, Chiltem St
London WIU 6NR

British Library Cataloguing in Publication Data

Ashworth, Leon
   William Shakespeare. – (British history makers)
   1.Shakespeare, William, 1564-1616 – Juvenile literature
   2. Dramatists, English – Early modern, 1500-1700 – Biography –
      Juvenile literature
   I.Title
   822.3'3

ISBN 1 84234 284 3

Printed and bound in Italy by Milanostampa - CN

First printed 1997. Reprinted 2005

Acknowledgments

Design: Richard Rowan
Editorial: John Grisewood
Artwork: Malcolm Porter
Photographs: *Barnaby's Picture Library* 4 bottom, 7 centre, 8 top & centre, 11
centre, 11 bottom (Courtesy of the Marquess of Salisbury), 15 bottom, 16
centre & bottom, 17 bottom left, 19 top & bottom right, 24 bottom, 25
bottom *The Bridgeman Art Library* 4 top, 9 centre, 9 bottom & back
cover (British Library, London), 10/11 top (The Royal Cornwall
Museum, Truro), 14 bottom, 19 bottom left (Dulwich Picture Gallery),
20 bottom & front cover, 23 top (Woburn Abbey, Bedfordshire)
& bottom (Forbes Magazine Collection, New York), 24 bottom
left (Victoria & Albert Museum, London), 25 centre, 26
bottom left (British Library, London), 28 bottom left *Corpus
Christi College, Cambridge (Courtesy of the Masters and
Fellows)* 17 bottom right *Dulwich Picture Gallery (By
permission of the trustees)* 12 left *e. t. archive* 13 centre, 20 top
Fitzwilliam Museum, University of Cambridge 12/13 bottom
Hulton Getty 21 centre *Jarrold Publishing* 26/27 centre, 27
bottom *The Mansell Collection* 6 top, 13 top, 21 bottom *Mary Evans Picture
Library* 16/17 top, 28 top, 29 top *National Portrait Gallery* 5 & cover
portrait, 18 left, 22 top *Public Record Office* 27 right *The Ronald Grant
Archive* 28 bottom right *Shakespeare's Globe/Richard Kalina* 29 centre &
bottom *Zefa* 6 bottom

CONTENTS

■ SHAKESPEARE — MAN OF THE THEATRE ■

WILLIAM SHAKESPEARE grew up in the England of Queen Elizabeth I and wrote his plays when the theatre was new. Now, more than 400 years later, these same plays still fill theatres with people who laugh at the jokes, cry at the sad parts, and marvel that one person could understand so much about human nature.

Shakespeare's was an exciting time to live. New ideas were in the air. There were new books to read. People were ready to fight over the rights and wrongs of religion. Travellers brought back tales of wonder from newly found lands overseas. Sailors told of their adventures in the Indies, Africa and America.

It was also a time when the wealthy and high-born took a keen interest in poetry, in art and in music. Famous adventurers and soldiers, such as Sir Walter Raleigh and Sir Philip Sidney, wrote poetry. Other wealthy people helped poets and artists by becoming their patrons – they paid and protected them.

Shakespeare's way of writing was new, too. Just seven years before he was born, the Earl of Surrey made up a new form of verse to turn Latin poems into English. It was called blank verse, and Shakespeare used blank verse for most of his plays.

Crowds flocked to the first theatres in Elizabeth's reign – and to keep them coming, the theatres needed new plays. William Shakespeare wrote them, and so successfully that they have kept the theatre alive to this day.

SHAKESPEARE'S LIFE

1564 *Shakespeare born*
1582 *Marries Anne Hathaway*
1583 *Daughter Susanna born*
1585 *Twins Hamnet and Judith born*
1590 *By now Shakespeare has left Stratford for London*
1596 *Son Hamnet dies*
1597 *Buys New Place in Stratford*
1616 *Shakespeare dies*

▲ **The poet Shakespeare dreams by the fire and, in this Victorian artist's fantasy, conjures out of the flames some of his best-known characters.**

▼ **Shakespeare's signature; one of six known examples, all of which are different. Experts claim that he used the spelling 'Shakspere'.**

4

Ben Jonson – poet, playwright and Shakespeare's friend – said *'He was not of an age, but for all time'*. Jonson also called Shakespeare *'Sweet Swan of Avon'*.

'All the world's a stage. And all the men and women merely players: They have their exits and their entrances; And one man in his time plays many parts.' Shakespeare *As You Like It*

■ THE SHAKESPEARE FAMILY ■

SHAKESPEARE'S BIRTH date is not known. He was christened in the church at Stratford-upon-Avon, Warwickshire, on 26 April 1564, when probably about three days old. Young William had a comfortable home in Henley Street. His father, John, was a glove-maker. His mother, Mary, was the daughter of a local farmer called Robert Arden.

SISTERS AND BROTHERS

William was the Shakespeares' first son. Two girls born before him both died in childhood. After him came two more sisters and three brothers. One of these sisters also died, aged eight. Edmund, the last brother, was born when William was 16.

A FATHER OF SOME IMPORTANCE

John Shakespeare was an important man in Stratford. Although he had once been fined for having a dunghill (rubbish dump) in front of his house, he had risen to a seat on the town council and was bailiff (mayor) when William was four. He may have had several business interests and certainly owned more than one house in the town. His own father, Richard, had been a farmer, renting land from the father of Mary Arden.

EVENTS

1564 Shakespeare born. Plague, brought to England by troops from France, reaches Stratford.
1565 John Shakespeare becomes an alderman in Stratford. Mary Queen of Scots marries Lord Darnley. Spanish found colony in Florida. First known use of pencils, in Switzerland.
1566 Mary Queen of Scots has a son, James (later James I of England). Riots between Protestants and Catholics in the Netherlands.
1567 Lord Darnley is blown up. Mary Queen of Scots marries the Earl of Bothwell.
1568 John Shakespeare is high bailiff (mayor) of Stratford. Mary Queen of Scots flees to England. War in Spanish Netherlands begins as Dutch fight for independence.

▲ The entry in the church register that records Shakespeare's christening is dated 26 April 1564, and his birthday is traditionally celebrated on 23 April.

▶ The font at which Shakespeare was christened is still in Holy Trinity Church, Stratford-upon-Avon. His father was an important man in the town so the family would have sat near the front at Sunday services.

▶ A plan of the house in Henley Street (far right) where Shakespeare was born. His father's trade in leather goods, wool and farm products was profitable enough for him to buy two houses in Stratford.

▼ Mary Arden's house at Wilmcote near Stratford. William's mother came from an old landowning family. She married John Shakespeare shortly after inheriting part of her father's property.

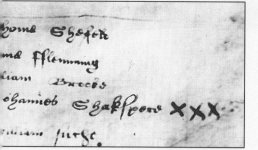

THE SHAKESPEARE CHILDREN

Joan, born 1558; dies before 1569, when another Joan is christened.
Margaret, born 1562; dies 1563.
William, born 1564; dies aged 52.

Joan, christened 1569; marries William Hart, a hatmaker; dies aged 77.
Gilbert, born 1566; dies aged 45.
Anne, born 1571; dies 1579.
Richard, born 1574; dies aged 38.
Edmund, born 1580; an actor; dies aged 27.

Town records tell us that John Shakespeare was a borough taster in 1556, with the job of inspecting Stratford's bread and ale. He also served for a time as constable, keeping law and order in the town, and was made an alderman (senior councillor) in 1565, soon after William was born. When plague struck Stratford around this time, the council met outdoors in an orchard – where they hoped to be safe from catching the deadly sickness.

■ SCHOOLDAYS AND AFTER ■

JOHN SHAKESPEARE, as an alderman, had the honour of wearing a fur-trimmed gown at big town events. He could also claim a free place for his son at the local grammar school. The schoolmaster, paid for by the council, taught the boys Latin, Greek, ancient history and rhetoric (the art of speech-making). Young Will would already have learned his alphabet from a 'hornbook' and his mother may have taught him how to read and write.

SPELL AS YOU LIKE IT

The grammar taught at Tudor grammar schools was Latin (the language of scholars throughout Europe). Anyone hoping for a career in the church, law or teaching had to read and write Latin correctly, but English did not follow such strict rules. Its spelling was not yet fixed, and people wrote words as they heard them.

School was hard work. The hours were long, holidays were few, and boys

EVENTS

1569 *The Queen's Players perform in Stratford's Guild Hall.*
1571 *A law requires all people over the age of seven in England to wear a woollen cap on Sundays – this is to boost trade for wool traders and cap-makers. Ottoman Turks lose sea battle of Lepanto to Don John of Austria.*
1572 *Government declares actors must be counted as 'sturdy beggars' unless licensed or under a lord's protection. The playwright Ben Jonson and poet John Donne are born. In France, over 20,000 Protestants (known as Huguenots) are killed in the St Bartholomew's Day Massacre.*

▲ **Bowls, or ninepins, was a popular game of skittles enjoyed by people of all classes.**

▶ **Twelfth Night – the last day of Christmas – was a time for revels and feasts.**

▲ **This may have been Shakespeare's schoolroom, but in his day there would have been no rows of desks. Only the master had a desk. The boys sat on benches and wrote on slates on their laps.**

◀ **Discipline was harsh in Tudor schools. Boys found playing about like these ones would have been beaten.**

who did not know their lessons were beaten. The playwright Ben Jonson said that the adult Shakespeare 'knew small Latin and less Greek'. The young Shakespeare may not have cared for the grammar of the ancient Greeks and Romans, but he liked their stories. Years later, he used them as plots for his plays.

FUN OUT OF SCHOOL

When not at school, young Will probably helped in the house and workshop. Perhaps he ran messages for his father, or visited his mother's farming relatives. There were country festivals and town fairs, the River Avon for swimming and fishing, and visits by strolling players or entertainers.

In 1569, the Queen's Players came to perform in Stratford's Guild Hall. They were a band of actors who performed 'Interludes', a mixture of long, high-flown speeches, funny cross-talk and slapstick comedy. Five-year-old Will Shakespeare may well have been allowed to watch their performances.

STROLLING PLAYERS

IN THE Middle Ages, people enjoyed plays put on by the craft guilds (such as the shoemakers or goldsmiths). These plays were Bible stories acted in the church porch or outside on a cart. By the time Shakespeare was a child, bands of actors and entertainers (below) were touring from town to town. Among them were clowns, acrobats, jugglers, singers and dancers. Some were regarded as little more than roving louts or beggars, but others were respectable. They performed in inn-yards, market places and streets, and sometimes in the halls of great houses. These actors usually had a nobleman as their patron and wore his livery (uniform). The best companies were famed countrywide – and even abroad.

■ MEETING THE PLAYERS ■

IN 1575, WHEN Will was 11, Stratford buzzed with excitement over Queen Elizabeth's visit to the Earl of Leicester at nearby Kenilworth Castle. For three weeks the queen's favourite courtier entertained her with dazzling displays of pageantry. News of the spectacular events no doubt prompted the Shakespeare family to walk from Stratford and see for themselves.

Will would not have been disappointed. The queen had brought her entire court. There was hunting and feasting; plays, pageants and masques on the castle lawns; fireworks at night; cannon-shooting by day; music, poetry and dancing. A display on the lake featured Orion the Hunter carrying off the Lady of the Lake on a dolphin.

Noble lords and ladies enjoyed dressing up to take part in pageants and masques. But the Earl of Leicester also had his own company of actors. Its leader was James Burbage, who in London was soon to open the first public theatre in England.

▲ A visit by Queen Elizabeth to nearby Kenilworth Castle would have been an occasion for everyone to remember. For most ordinary local people it would have been a once-in-a-lifetime chance to glimpse the splendour of the monarch and her courtiers.

▼ Anne Hathaway's Cottage at Shottery near Stratford was the farmhouse in which Shakespeare's wife lived before their marriage. This event took place by special licence soon after the death of her father. The licence allowed couples to marry without the customary calling of banns.

CHANGING CIRCUMSTANCES

By 1580 Will Shakespeare had left school. His young sister Anne had just died and his last brother Edmund was newly born. Family life was not so easy now. John Shakespeare had money problems. He sold land, was excused paying taxes and lost his place on the town council. William did not go to university. He may have found work as a teacher or in a lawyer's office, or with his father. He had to earn money somehow, for in 1582 at the age of 18 he was married and a year later he was a father.

Will's wife, Anne Hathaway, was a farmer's daughter and eight years older than her husband. Their first child was called Susanna. Twins were born two years later in 1585, a girl, Judith, and a boy, Hamnet.

▼ **Servants prepare a feast as musicians play and wedding guests stroll and chat. This picture, called A Fête at Bermondsey, is by the Dutch painter Hoefnagel.**

NOBLE COMPANY OF ACTORS

IN 1572, the government passed a law for the 'Punishment of Vagabonds'. In future, such wanderers as pedlars, jugglers, tinkers (pot-menders), chapmen (street sellers), fencers (sword-fighters) and common players (actors) would be treated as 'sturdy beggars'. This meant that they could be whipped back to their home parish (above), unless they had a licence or were employed by a nobleman. Players rushed to join the professional acting companies of a nobleman and wear his livery.

■ SEEKING HIS FORTUNE ■

THE EARL OF Leicester was not the only nobleman with his own company of actors. The earls of Worcester, Warwick and Berkeley all had companies that performed in Stratford while Shakespeare was there. Worcester's men had by far the finest actor, Edward Alleyn, who was just two years younger than Shakespeare. Perhaps while watching or talking to the players – helping or writing something topical about Stratford for them – young Will discovered that performing plays was what he wanted to do. But where was he to do it? And how?

JOINING A COMPANY

Sometime in the late 1580s, William Shakespeare decided to leave Stratford and seek his fortune in London, as others had done before him. He

◀ **Edward Alleyn, the finest actor of his day. He owned several theatres and organized bull- and bear-baiting events. He made so much money that he was able to found Dulwich College school.**

▶ **On the bank of the River Thames at Richmond, morris dancers perform and collect money from wealthy passers-by.**

CLOWN AND JESTER

YOUNG Shakespeare in Stratford probably laughed when he saw the clown Richard Tarlton (right) poking his head around a curtain, cross-eyed and pulling faces, or capering about playing a pipe and tabor (small drum). Like all writers, Will later made use of his memories in his work. When he first came to London, Tarlton may still have been on the stage. He was a favourite court jester of Queen Elizabeth and many of his tricks were copied by later clowns. Tarlton died in 1588. It is probable that he was recalled by Shakespeare as Yorick, the dead jester in *Hamlet* who had made the young prince laugh.

may have left with an acting company. The Queen's Men who played in Stratford in 1587 had just lost an actor, killed in a stabbing. Two of their other players were famous comedians: the young Will Kemp and Richard Tarlton, a clown and entertainer near the end of his career. Will Shakespeare may have joined them as an apprentice.

LEAVING FOR THE CITY

Very little is known about Shakespeare's life at this time. For years there was a story that he fled Stratford after being caught poaching deer from Sir Thomas Lucy. Few people now believe this. Other tales tell of him working in Gloucestershire as a tutor to the Earl of Berkeley's children, or as a soldier abroad. All we do know is that by 1592, William Shakespeare was making his living by writing plays in London.

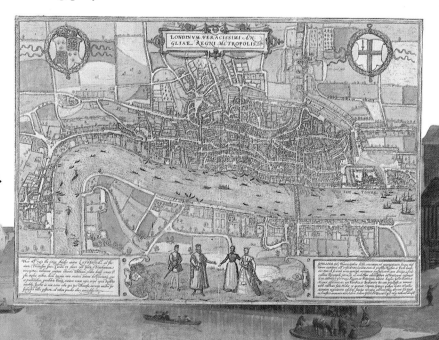

▶ **A map of London, drawn in 1572, shows its densely packed streets, and river busy with traffic.**

■ THE ROAD TO LONDON ■

SHAKESPEARE travelled the road between Stratford and London many times. Journeys then were on horseback or on foot. Only the queen and the very rich had carriages. People rested and ate at wayside inns, if they could afford to. Others found or begged shelter where they could.

A MAGNET FOR ALL SORTS

When young Will reached London in the 1580s, he found a crowded, dirty city that was full of life, sounds and action. It was a busy port, huddled beside the River Thames, its streets thronged with people of all sorts and trades. Trade was nowhere brisker than in the ale-houses, where inn-keepers found entertainers good for business. Plays and mimes (called dumb-shows) were acted in the yards of city taverns, but the crowds they attracted also brought pickpockets and cutpurses, drunkards and beggars.

▲ One of London's large inns. The throng of people was a lure for players and pickpockets alike.

▼ A picture map of London in the 1600s, showing the Globe theatre (bottom right). Across the Thames is the old St Paul's Cathedral. This, and most of the other buildings on the north side, was destroyed in the Great Fire of 1666.

A BUMPY RIDE

WHEN Queen Elizabeth travelled about her kingdom, she took with her 400 wagons full of belongings. Poor people went with their goods in heavy wooden carts pulled by up to ten horses. Tudor coaches had no springs and were very uncomfortable – the queen rode in one only when entering a town. Most travellers hired horses at each inn they stopped at. Roads were rarely mended and ruts made by cart wheels were so deep that people sometimes fell into them and drowned. Carts often turned over. There were no road signs and farmers sometimes ploughed across the highway. Nobody dared travel at night for fear of robbers hiding in the woods. When they stopped at inns, they were preyed upon by cutpurses (right).

▼ 'Bring out your dead!' During the plague years, carts rolled through the streets of London collecting bodies for burial. The disease spread rapidly through the hot city streets with their cramped dwellings. Actors complained that the theatres were closed, but during 1593 alone, the disease killed 11,000 Londoners.

A DANGER TO MORALS AND HEALTH

Plays, according to the strict, religious Puritans, were 'the nest of the Devil and the sink of all sin'. London's Lord Mayor also thought plays were dangerous because of 'sundry slaughters and maimings of the queen's subjects, that have happened by falling scaffolds, frames and stages, and by engines, weapons and powder used in plays'. Special effects obviously went wrong! Crowded audiences were breeding grounds, too, for the plague and other diseases.

LONDON'S NEW THEATRES

When plague struck London in hot summers, all performances of plays were stopped and the actors left town to tour the country. Complaints about the players and their rowdy audiences soon brought more rules and regulations from the Lord Mayor. Life became so difficult for actors in the city that they decided to move outside it.

James Burbage, actor to the Earl of Leicester and the queen, rented some ground in grassy Shoreditch and there built a 'plaie howse' of wood. Burbage, a trained carpenter, called it the Theatre (short for amphitheatre) and opened it in 1576. It did so well that the following year another playhouse, called the Curtain, opened nearby. Soon a rival playhouse, the Rose, was opened by Philip Henslowe. When Shakespeare came to London, these theatres were all thriving.

■ ACTOR AND PLAYWRIGHT ■

S HAKESPEARE probably learned his acting skills with Burbage's company at the Theatre. There was also a story that he began work in London *outside* the theatre – looking after the horses of rich members of the audience while they were inside watching the play!

Playgoers making for the Rose theatre crossed the Thames by ferry. Nearby stood the Bear Garden, where people watched mastiff dogs set upon a bear or a bull tied to a post. Other popular sports were cock-fighting, wrestling and bowls matches. Archers shot at targets at the butts, in fields near the city.

Rival attractions like these made theatres work hard to keep their customers. Besides plays, they put on variety and circus acts, and often ended the entertainment with a 'jig' – a knockabout farce with jokes, cross-talk, topical satire and spirited dancing presented by the clowns.

HITS OF THE DAY
Acting companies sent spies to watch

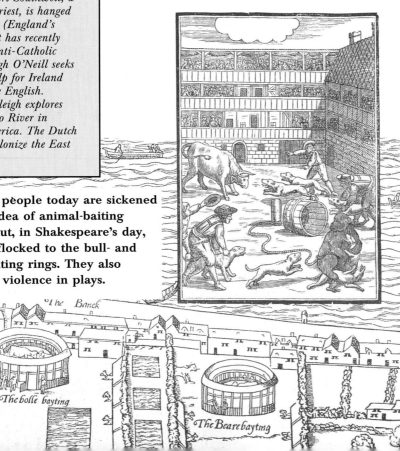

▼ Most people today are sickened by the idea of animal-baiting (right) but, in Shakespeare's day, crowds flocked to the bull- and bear-baiting rings. They also enjoyed violence in plays.

THE THEATRE

P UBLIC theatres like the Swan (above) put on shows in the daytime only. The buildings were round, square or many sided, and open to the sky. Most had three-tiered galleries built round a courtyard known as the pit. Customers stood in the pit, or paid extra to sit on benches in the galleries. The standing spectators were called groundlings. At one end the apron stage jutted out over the pit. Actors came and went through doorways at the back of the stage. Behind these were the dressing rooms. The stage had a trap door (through which devils

new plays put on by their rivals. They wrote down as much as they could of the words and plot in shorthand and then produced their own 'pirate' version. Shakespeare probably saw many of the new plays written by clever young men called the 'university wits'. Their pieces mixed poetry and low comedy, romance and rhetoric. The best plays were those by Christopher Marlowe, whose *Tamburlaine*, *The Jew of Malta* and *Dr Faustus* were all acted by Edward Alleyn. Marlowe's friend Thomas Kyd wrote a popular play called *The Spanish Tragedy*. Audiences loved this tale of horror, with its ghosts, gory murders, torture and madness.

A NEW AUTHOR MAKES A MARK

Some of these early playwrights led dangerous, violent lives themselves. Marlowe, a spy in the government's secret service, was killed in a tavern brawl. His friend and fellow playwright Robert Greene kept company with thieves and vagabonds, and died in poverty. Just before his death in 1592, Greene warned playwrights against a newcomer – an 'upstart crow' who thought himself able to write blank verse as well as the university men. He was 'in his own conceit the only "Shakes-scene" in a country'. Greene was writing about William Shakespeare.

In 1592, Philip Henslowe put on a new play – *Harry the Sixth* – at the Rose. It made more money than anything else played all season. We know the play as Shakespeare's *Henry VI*. Shakespeare the actor was now a playwright.

▼ A page from the prompt book for *Titus Andronicus* shows the costumes that actors wore in Shakespeare's time.

▼ This may be a portrait of Christopher Marlowe, the greatest English playwright before Shakespeare.

and ghosts could appear and disappear). Sound and other special effects were worked from the hut, which stood on top of the 'heavens', a half-roof over the stage. Machinery inside could let down an actor from the 'sky'. There was no curtain or scenery, but actors did use props such as crowns, swords, furniture and artificial trees which were kept in the tiring-house on each tier. To advertise the play, a flag was hoisted over the theatre to show that a performance would take place in the afternoon. To announce the start, there was much blowing of trumpets, ringing of bells and banging of drums.

■ PLAYS AND PLAYERS ■

SHAKESPEARE had probably written his first plays by 1589-90, perhaps while still learning the actor's trade. Among the earliest were *The Comedy of Errors*, *The Taming of the Shrew* and *Richard III*. Then in 1593 plague struck London. The theatres were shut and many players left to tour the country or act abroad. Shakespeare seems to have stayed in the city and, as no new plays were needed, he wrote poems instead. Poets in Elizabethan England commanded more respect than playwrights.

EVENTS

1596 Shakespeare's son Hamnet dies. The Shakespeares gain a coat of arms. The Swan theatre is built on the south bank of the Thames, seating 3000. Shakespeare is involved in a lawsuit. Drake dies in the West Indies. Edmund Spenser publishes his epic poem The Faerie Queene. *1597* Ben Jonson begins acting and writing. James Burbage dies. Shakespeare buys New Place in Stratford. A new Poor Law makes parishes responsible for looking after the local poor. Rebellion in Ireland.

PUBLISHED POEMS

Shakespeare wrote two long poems, *Venus and Adonis* and *The Rape of Lucrece*. He dedicated them both to the young Earl of Southampton, probably in return for gifts of money. Both were printed by Richard Field, a neighbour from Stratford who was now a printer in London. These poems were the only works by Shakespeare that he published himself.

◀ The Earl of Southampton was Shakespeare's patron, though nobody knows exactly how much money he paid to the poet or how well the two men knew each other. It is possible that Shakespeare lived in his household for a time.

▶ A list made in Shakespeare's day of some of the actors who performed in his plays.

SHAKESPEARE'S ACTORS

THERE were no actresses in Shakespeare's day. All parts were taken by men, with boys or youths playing women and children. Companies had around eight to twelve 'sharers' who ran the business and were the leading actors. They employed hirelings to do odd jobs, play music or act as prompts (whispering the next line if an actor forgot his words). The Lord Chamberlain's Men were originally Will Kemp and Thomas Pope (both clowns), John Heminges, Augustine Phillips and George Bryan. Burbage and Shakespeare then joined them. Kemp probably played Bottom the Weaver in *A Midsummer Night's Dream*.

▼ The clown Robert Armin had a good voice, so Shakespeare wrote songs for him to sing in the plays.

SHAKESPEARE'S SONNETS

SHAKESPEARE was a superb poet. He wrote a series of 154 short poems, or sonnets, before 1600. A sonnet is a poem of 14 lines, and many famous people of Shakespeare's day, such as Sir Philip Sidney and Sir Walter Raleigh, wrote sonnets. Among Shakespeare's most famous is the one that begins *'Shall I compare thee to a summer's day . . .'* The first 126 sonnets are addressed to a young nobleman; the rest are apparently written to a woman. We do not know who these people were. The sonnets were printed in 1609.

▲ Richard Burbage.

▶ A drawing of New Place, Shakespeare's house in Stratford. The building itself has long gone.

BACK IN BUSINESS

In 1594 the theatres opened again. Shakespeare's fellow actors regrouped and found a new patron: the Lord Chamberlain. In October 1594 they opened at the Theatre in Shoreditch, led by Richard Burbage, son of James. Shakespeare was now an important member of the Lord Chamberlain's Men, a 'sharer' (shareholder) taking part of the profits. He worked hard, producing about two plays a year. All were written to suit the members of the company – with parts for each actor.

HEROES AND CLOWNS

Richard Burbage took the leads as Hamlet, Othello, Macbeth or King Lear. Comic parts went to Will Kemp until he left the company in 1599. This cheerful clown, singer and dancer had played in the lively comedies *A Midsummer Night's Dream* and *Much Ado About Nothing.* For Kemp's replacement, Robert Armin, Shakespeare wrote more thoughtful parts in *As You Like It* and *Twelfth Night.* Even in his tragedies, Shakespeare wrote funny scenes for his leading comic to play.

A 'GENTLEMAN'

By 1598, Shakespeare had written over a dozen plays. They were performed for the queen at court, as well as in the theatre, and made him wealthy enough to buy New Place – the second-biggest house in Stratford. It cost him £60 in 1597. A year earlier, he had helped his father pay for a coat of arms and with it the formal status of a 'gentleman'. The actor and playwright was now entitled to be called Mr Shakespeare. But the honour would not pass to William's son, for in August 1596, young Hamnet Shakespeare died.

■ AROUND THE GLOBE ■

THE LORD Chamberlain's Men were soon London's most successful company, but they badly needed a new building. Their lease on the Theatre was running out. At last, the company found a new site at Bankside in Southwark. In the bitter cold of Christmas 1598, they tore down the old Theatre building and carted its timbers across the frozen Thames.

The new theatre was London's finest. Large enough to hold perhaps 2500 people, it was round so the actors named it the Globe. On the flag that fluttered from its roof was the motto (in Latin) 'All the world's a stage'.

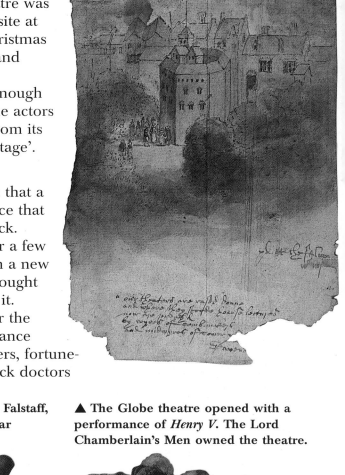

EVENTS
. . . .

1598 *Shakespeare acts in Ben Jonson's play* Every Man in His Humour. *Jonson kills a fellow-actor in a duel and is sent to prison. King Philip II of Spain dies.*
1599 *The Globe theatre opens. The Earl of Essex is sent to deal with the rebels in Ireland, but fails.*
1600 *The East India Company is founded, for trade with Asia.*
1604 *Shakespeare is staying with the Mountjoys in Cripplegate.*

INSIDE THE GLOBE

The flag was raised as a sign that a performance would take place that afternoon, starting at 2 o'clock. Each play was performed for a few days, and then replaced with a new one – though it would be brought back later if audiences liked it. People paid a penny to enter the theatre, and around the entrance were sideshows where jugglers, fortune-tellers, apple-sellers and quack doctors

▼ **Hogarth's painting of Sir John Falstaff, one of Shakespeare's most popular characters.**

▲ **The Globe theatre opened with a performance of *Henry V*. The Lord Chamberlain's Men owned the theatre.**

How Actors Spoke and Acted

SHAKESPEARE'S actors probably spoke quickly, in a clear, musical style. They would not have sounded like actors today. The actors' accents included ones that may have sounded like those of Lancashire, America or Ireland today. 'Love' and 'above', for example, rhymed with 'prove' and 'move', and the *ea* sound in 'reason' sounded like the *ea* in 'steak'.

▶ There were no drama schools, so actors learned from one another; set gestures (above)

reinforced their words. A clenched fist indicated pain, a scratched head puzzlement and so on.

touted for more coins.

Inside, the audience chatted cheerfully as they waited for the trumpet blast that signalled the start of the play. Playhouses were noisy. Audiences clapped what they liked and 'mewed' what they did not. After the play came the jig – comic turns and dancing.

On the stage of the Globe, Shakespeare's greatest plays had their first performances. He had been writing more about English history, creating in *Henry IV* (Parts 1 & 2) the part of the fat, drunken Sir John Falstaff – a great favourite with audiences and with Queen Elizabeth.

A family friendship

Like the theatre, Shakespeare too seems to have moved. For some years he lodged in the house of a Huguenot (French Protestant) family called Mountjoy in Silver Street, Cripplegate. Maybe he found them helpful with the French spoken in the Globe's opening play, *Henry V*. If so, Shakespeare returned the favour by helping the Mountjoys arrange a marriage for their daughter. We know this because in 1612, he was asked to give evidence when a dispute over the wedding agreement came to court. Shakespeare's evidence favoured neither one side nor the other. People seem to have found him a 'gentle' (meaning polite and tactful) man.

▲ Ben Jonson was a friend and admirer of Shakespeare, and the two men acted in each other's plays.

▶ Will Kemp, accompanied by his piper Thomas Sly, soon left the Globe. He laid a bet that he would dance all the way from London to Norwich. 'Kemp's jig' took nine days. Crowds watched him pass; he gained the freedom of Norwich, a life pension, and wrote a book. Following this success he left England to dance on the Continent, returning in 1602 to act for the Earl of Worcester's Men.

■ THE KING'S MEN ■

MANY OF Shakespeare's plays, even those about English or Roman history, refer to topical events and famous people of the day. Sometimes the players themselves were caught up in these events. Queen Elizabeth was growing old. The Earl of Essex, her former favourite, felt himself badly treated by the queen and government after failing on a mission to Ireland. In 1601, Essex led a revolt. On the day of the uprising, his supporters paid the Lord Chamberlain's Men to act Shakespeare's *Richard II*, a play about a king's overthrow. The revolt failed. Essex was beheaded. The actors were questioned, but not punished.

▲ **King James I.**

A MAN OF SUBSTANCE

Old John Shakespeare died the same year (1601), having lived to see his son restore the family fortune and honour by the skill of his pen. William inherited the house in Henley Street.

TRICKS OF THE TRADE

AUDIENCES loved exciting special effects, such as sparks and thunderbolts, cannon, drums, flags, fights and processions. The shouts and trumpets of a stage battle could be heard across the river! Actors dressed behind the stage. They put on wigs and make-up – flour to whiten the face, ink to draw lines, brick-dust for red cheeks, burnt cork and charcoal for black faces and shadows. Blood came from the butcher, and splendid costumes were often bought secondhand from noblemen and women. A property list of Philip Henslowe's includes: '1 lion skin; 1 bear's skin; Neptune's fork and garland; Kent's wooden leg'. It also includes a 'frame for the heading' – trick machinery for making it look as though an actor's head had been cut off!

BOY-ACTORS

THERE were two famous all-boy acting companies: the Children of St Paul's and the Children of the Chapel Royal. As well as performing plays, they were choirboys, singing and reciting verses at court. In fact, they became serious rivals to the men's companies. The boy-actors (right) did not perform in public, but played to select audiences in candlelit halls, where scenes of bloody murder and ghostly apparitions went down well in the shadows. Talented boys were sometimes kidnapped to join the companies!

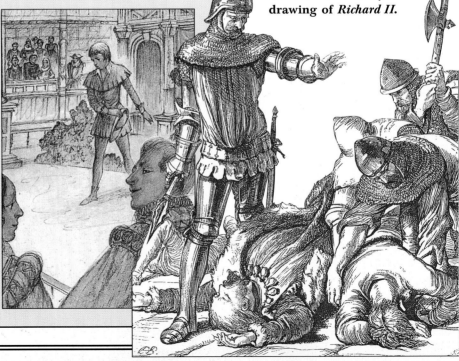

▼ **The death of the king, from a 19th-century drawing of *Richard II*.**

▲ In masques, lavish costumes, scenery and spectacle were more important than words.

▼ A 19th-century painting of *As You Like It*. In Shakespeare's day, the girls would have been played by boys.

By now he was a wealthy man, with land and investments in Stratford and London. Two years later, in 1603, Queen Elizabeth died and the Scottish king James VI came to England to take the throne. James loved the theatre and granted the Lord Chamberlain's Men a royal charter. From now on they were The King's Men. Their foremost members, including Shakespeare, became Grooms of the Bedchamber – an honorary position at court.

A COUNTRY OUTING

Plague again hit London in 1603 and the actors left town. They were commanded to appear before King James at Wilton House near Salisbury, home of the countess of Pembroke. Family tradition has it that on 3 December they played *As You Like It* and that the countess wrote in a letter 'We have the man Shakespeare with us'. The actors were paid £30. Shakespeare was a good actor, by all accounts, but usually took small parts such as the Ghost in *Hamlet*, old men and kings. He would have been a good understudy, since he knew everyone's lines!

ROBED FOR THE BEDCHAMBER

When James was crowned in 1604, Shakespeare walked in the coronation procession through London wearing his Groom of the Bedchamber red livery. The playwright's name headed the list of actors supplied with four and a half yards of red cloth for the occasion by the Master of the Great Wardrobe.

Over Christmas 1604, James saw his King's Men in eight of Shakespeare's plays, including *Othello* at the Banqueting House in Whitehall, *The Merry Wives of Windsor* and *Measure for Measure*. In spring, he saw *Love's Labour's Lost*, *Henry V* and *Measure for Measure*.

■ END OF THE GLOBE ■

BETWEEN 1604 and 1608, Shakespeare wrote his greatest tragedies: *Othello, King Lear, Macbeth, Antony and Cleopatra* and *Coriolanus. Macbeth*, a play about Scottish history, was no doubt written with King James in mind. The king was a superstitious man, fascinated by witchcraft. In the play, Macbeth is drawn on to kill King Duncan by three witches. Guy Fawkes and his fellow conspirators had just tried to blow up James – a fate that had befallen the king's father, Lord Darnley.

BROTHERS AND PARTNERS

William was not the only Shakespeare in London. His brother Gilbert was a haberdasher (clothes-seller) there, but, like William, kept his old links with Stratford. Younger brother Edmund had become an actor, but not with William's company. He died in London in 1607.

In 1608 Shakespeare's company took over an indoor theatre – the Blackfriars – which they could use during the winter. It had formerly

▼ **Striking terror into his murderer, the ghost of Banquo appears ingeniously out of a pillar in this Victorian production of Shakespeare's tragedy *Macbeth*.**

THE PLAYS

THE DATES are those of the likely first performance of the plays. There is not enough evidence for scholars to be able to agree on actual dates.
1589-91 *Henry VI* (three parts)
1593 *Richard III, The Comedy of Errors*
1594 *Titus Andronicus, The Taming of the Shrew, Two Gentlemen of Verona, Love's Labour's Lost, Romeo and Juliet*
1595 *Richard II, A Midsummer Night's Dream*
1596 *King John, The Merchant of Venice*
1597 *Henry IV* (parts 1 and 2)

▶ **The great 18th-century actor David Garrick introduced a more 'natural' style of acting and helped rekindle interest in Shakespeare. Here he is shown playing four of the great tragic heroes.**

▼ **An indoor playhouse. This 17th-century drawing shows many of the characters and 'turns' that appeared on the stage. Unlike the sunlit open-air theatres, indoor playhouses had chandeliers and footlights to light performances at night.**

LEAR.   MACBETH.

RICHARD III.   HAMLET.

Mʳ GARRICK in Four of his Principal Tragic Characters.

been used by a company of child-actors, who were popular with fashionable audiences. A new theatre meant more new plays, and now Francis Beaumont and John Fletcher began to write for the King's Men. Fletcher later replaced Shakespeare as the company playwright. The two worked together on *Henry VIII*.

TIME TO GO?

By 1609 Shakespeare was thinking of leaving London, and three years later was back in Stratford, though still writing from time to time. He also kept a business interest in London, buying a house in Blackfriars which he let out. One of his business partners was the landlord of the Mermaid Tavern, where poets and playwrights met to eat, drink and talk. Ben Jonson, John Donne, Beaumont, Fletcher and Sir Walter Raleigh all went there. Shakespeare was famous and popular. *Hamlet* and *Richard II* were even played on board a ship bound for the East Indies in 1607-08. His new plays *The Tempest* and *The Winter's Tale* were played before the king in 1611.

A FIERY END

Shakespeare's play-writing career probably ended when the Globe did. The theatre went out with a bang. On 29 June 1613, *Henry VIII* was in full swing. A cannon was fired and its paper 'shot' set fire to the thatched roof. The blaze destroyed the Globe in less than an hour.

Shakespeare's theatre was gone. Its timbers – as part of the old Theatre – had resounded to his first plays and – as part of the Globe – to his last. When the rebuilt Globe reopened, Shakespeare was back home in Stratford.

▼ A model of the Globe and its surroundings. Amazingly, no lives were lost as the 2000-strong audience fled the burning building in 1613. Fire ripped through the thatched roof but the oak timbers were slower to flame.

■ BACK TO STRATFORD ■

SHAKESPEARE had eased gently into retirement. He kept his interests in London and the theatre, and friends came to visit him in Stratford. In April 1616, Ben Jonson paid him a call. The poet Michael Drayton, who lived nearby, joined them in a 'merrie meeting' at which they drank wine and ate pickled herrings.

Then Shakespeare fell ill. He made his will, and died on 23 April, aged 52. The parish register records the burial two days later of 'Will. Shakespeare, gent.'.

WILL AND HIS PLAYS

Shakespeare left most of his property to his daughter Susanna. He also left small sums to Stratford friends and three in London, including Richard Burbage. He left his wife the 'second-best bed' but by law she would have had a share of the property too.

By 1619, pirated copies of Shakespeare's plays were being printed. The King's Men put a stop to this and determined to have them published accurately. John Heminges and Henry Condell, the actor friends left money by Shakespeare, gathered together his writings and

Mr. WILLIAM
SHAKESPEARES
COMEDIES, HISTORIES, & TRAGEDIES.
Published according to the True Originall Copies.

LONDON
Printed by Isaac Iaggard, and Ed. Blount. 1623.

◀ The title page of the First Folio, printed in 1623. Gathering the texts of so many plays, and then separating bad pirated texts from true versions was a labour of love for Shakespeare's friends, John Heminges and Henry Condell.

IVDICIO PYLIVM GENIO SOCRATEM ARTE
TERRA TEGIT, POPVLVS MÆRET, OLYM

STAY PASSENGER, WHY GOEST THOV BY
READ IF THOV CANST, WHOM ENVIOVS DEATH
WITH IN THIS MONVMENT SHAKSPEARE, WITH
QVICK NATVRE DIDE WHOSE NAME, DOTH DECK Y
FAR MORE THEN COST: SIEH ALL Y HE HATH
LEAVES LIVING ART, BVT PAGE, TO SERVE HI

WHO WAS SHAKESPEARE?

SHAKESPEARE'S plays show such a wide interest and knowledge of the world, and of human nature, that people are amazed they could be the work of one man – and a man with only a free grammar school education. Some doubters have claimed that the plays were written by Christopher Marlowe (after a fake 'death'), by the statesman Francis Bacon, the Earl of Southampton or other noblemen. Some even claim that Queen Elizabeth herself wrote them! The most convincing theory is that Shakespeare's plays were written by Shakespeare.

◀ **This monument to Shakespeare was built near his tomb in Holy Trinity Church a few years after his death. Memorials in Stratford today include several working theatres.**

▶ **Shakespeare wrote his will about a month before his death. He left his home to his daughter, Susanna, but his wife Anne would have continued to live there.**

▼ **Because of the curse inscribed on his tomb, some people think that a secret lies hidden in Shakespeare's grave. It is more likely that he simply did not want people to disturb his bones.**

produced the First Folio of all the plays in 1623 in order 'to keep the memory of so worthy a friend and fellow alive'.

WHAT WAS HE LIKE?

Before Shakespeare's wife Anne died in 1623, a monument to Will had been put up in Stratford church, with a bust of the playwright. People who knew Shakespeare said it was like him. The portrait of him in the First Folio is also said to be a good likeness. The picture known as the Chandos portrait (see page 5) was owned by Shakespeare's godson and may have been painted by Richard Burbage.

From Heminges and Condell, who collected his work, we learn that Shakespeare's 'mind and hand went together; and what he thought, he uttered with that easinesse that we have scarce received from him a blot in his papers'.

GOOD FREND FOR IESVS SAKE FORBEARE,
TO DIGG THE DVST ENCLOASED HEARE:
BLESE BE Y MAN Y SPARES THES STONES,
AND CVRST BE HE Y MOVES MY BONES.

■ SHAKESPEARE'S LEGACY ■

NEARLY FOUR hundred years after his death, Shakespeare keeps the theatre alive. He gives work to actors, writers, directors, painters, technicians and all who work to put on his plays – on the stage, on television and in the cinema. Even when set at other periods of history or staged in modern dress, Shakespeare's plays still make sense. His lines are spoken all over the world, in many languages.

Thousands of tourists flock each year to see where he lived in Stratford and to watch the plays at the theatres there. There are Shakespeare festivals, Shakespeare seasons, Shakespeare souvenirs. There is a reconstruction of the Globe theatre in London, close to the site of the original.

Shakespeare is the world's greatest playwright and probably the greatest-ever writer. We know little of his life but know what his mind could imagine. He used more English words than any other writer in the language, and made up many of his own. Phrases we use in everyday speech – quick as a flash, light as air, blood burns, cold comfort, small beer, blinking idiot, and many many more – were coined by Shakespeare. People who have never seen or read his plays may quote from them daily.

▲▼ Shakespeare's characters fascinate actors and audiences alike. Many people visit each new production of a play to see how a particular director and cast interpret it. Among famous actors to have played *Richard III* are Edmund Kean (above), David Garrick (below left) and, on stage and film in our own time, Ian McKellen (below).

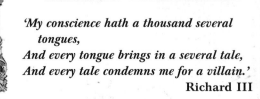

'My conscience hath a thousand several tongues,
And every tongue brings in a several tale,
And every tale condemns me for a villain.'
Richard III

SHAKESPEARE IN OUR LANGUAGE

QUOTATIONS

My salad days . . . Antony and Cleopatra
Brevity is the soul of wit . . .
Neither a borrower nor a lender be . . . Hamlet
This was the most unkindest cut of all . . . Julius Caesar
So shines a good deed in a naughty world . . . Merchant of Venice
Pomp and circumstance . . .
I will wear my heart upon my sleeve . . . Othello
O brave new world . . . The Tempest
If music be the food of love, play on . . . Twelfth Night
And thereby hangs a tale . . . As You Like It

EVERYDAY PHRASES

I have not slept one wink. Cymbeline
More in sorrow than in anger.
Time is out of joint.
Cruel only to be kind. Hamlet
All our yesterdays.
What's done is done.
(He hath) eaten me out of house and home. Macbeth
Men of few words. Henry V
It was Greek to me. Julius Caesar
But love is blind. Merchant of Venice
What's in a name? Romeo and Juliet
Cold comfort King John

◀ **Shakespeare's monument in Westminster Abbey. His living memorial is the richness of the English language.**

▼ **A new Globe. Audiences can relive the experience of Shakespeare's theatre at the reconstructed Globe, built near the site of the original. It opened in** 1997 **with a production of** *Henry V*, **as did the old Globe in 1599. Modern groundlings (right) stand where their forerunners did, in the pit.**

■ GLOSSARY ■

ALDERMAN A senior member of a town council, elected by other members usually after long service.

APPRENTICE A young man learning a trade; an apprenticeship in the service of an experienced master could last up to seven years.

APRON In the theatre, part of the stage that sticks out in front of the arch.

BAILIFF A land-agent or estate manager.

BAITING Letting dogs fight tethered bulls or bears for entertainment.

BANNS Public announcement of a proposed wedding, read out in church.

BLANK VERSE Unrhymed verse with lines of five two-syllable 'feet'.

BOROUGH TASTER Town official whose job was to check the quality of local bread and other foods.

BUTTS Mounds behind targets.

CHAPMEN A travelling seller of cheap goods.

CLOWN In Shakespeare's time, clown could mean a country simpleton or a professional comedian.

COMPANY A group of actors working, and travelling, together.

CONSTABLE A local law officer, rather like a village policeman.

COURT The people who live and work with a monarch, and the royal buildings.

COURTIER Member of the court, usually a noble.

CROSSTALK Quickfire conversation between two actors, usually full of jokes.

CUTPURSE A pickpocket or street thief.

DEDICATE To set apart something for a purpose; to address a book or play to an individual, as a mark of respect.

DUMB-SHOW Play without words, mimes.

DUNGHILL A rubbish heap, where human waste might (or might not) be left.

FENCERS Sword-fighters, people who show off their swordsmanship.

GRAMMAR Rules of language and writing.

GRAMMAR SCHOOL Boys' schools in Tudor England, where Latin grammar was taught, and from which many later schools evolved.

GREEK Language spoken in Greece; in Shakespeare's time, scholars studied the language of the Ancient Greeks.

GROUNDLINGS People who paid the cheapest prices to stand in a theatre.

GUILD An association of craftsmen or merchants to which the different craftsmen and merchants had to belong to obtain work in a town.

GUILD HALL Building put up by a guild for its meeting and banquets.

HABERDASHER A dealer in ribbons and small items of clothing.

HORNBOOK A child's schoolbook, made from a single sheet protected by transparent horn.

HUGUENOTS French Protestants, some of whom sought refuge in England from religious persecution.

INN A place where travellers could stay, often built around an open courtyard.

LATIN Language of Ancient Romans, still used in Shakespeare's time as the language of scholars.

LICENCE Permit needed for various purposes, including the performance of a play or for a marriage.

LIVERY Distinctive uniforms worn by servants of a great household or by members of a guild.

LORD CHAMBERLAIN The person responsible for entertainment at court.

LORD MAYOR The chief citizen of London and other important cities; the elected leader of the council.

MASQUES Entertainments with songs, music and acting, often performed in great houses.

NOBLE A person from a rich or important family usually with a title, such as Duke, Earl, Lord, etc.

PAGEANT A dramatic entertainment, often to mark some important event, when people dress up to re-enact stories from history.

PATRONS Rich people who encourage artists and writers by giving them employment or paying for plays to be put on and poems published.

PIT The ground floor of a theatre

PLAGUE A deadly contagious disease carried by fleas from black rats; epidemics of plague killed thousands of people from the 14th to the 17th centuries.

PLAYER Actor.

PLAYHOUSE Theatre.

POACHING Illegally hunting game animals, such as rabbits or deer.

PROPS Short for properties; stage equipment, such as furniture and weapons, that can be moved about.

PURITAN A Christian who follows a simple way of life and a strict form of worship.

QUACK Short for quacksalver, a fake doctor who sold useless medicines (salves), claiming miracle cures for almost anything.

SHARER A person who invests money in a theatre or other venture in return for a share of the profits.

SHORTHAND Quick form of writing.

SPANISH ARMADA Invasion fleet sent by Spain to attack England.

STROLLING PLAYER An actor who wandered from town to town.

TABOR A small drum; the player struck the tabor with one hand, while playing a pipe held in the other.

TIRING HOUSE Room in which actors dressed for the play and stored props.

TOUR To go from town to town performing plays.

TUDOR Family name of the dynasty to which Elizabeth I belonged, founded by Henry VII.

TUTOR A private teacher, employed to teach children at home.

TYBURN Place of execution in London, where Marble Arch now stands.

UNDERSTUDY Actor who learns another's part so that he or she can act as a stand-in.

PLACES TO VISIT

Any performance of any Shakespeare play anywhere.

Anne Hathaway's Cottage,
Shottery, Warwickshire.
Home of Shakespeare's bride.

Hall's Croft,
Stratford-upon-Avon, Warwickshire
Home of Shakespeare's daughter.

Holy Trinity Church,
Stratford-upon-Avon, Warwickshire.

International Shakespeare's Globe Centre,
Bankside, London.
This includes the Globe theatre, exhibition and education department.

Mary Arden's House and Shakespeare Countryside Museum,
Wilmcote, Warwickshire.
Home of Shakespeare's mother.

Nash's House and New Place,
Stratford-upon-Avon, Warwickshire.
Site and grounds of Shakespeare's last house.

National Portrait Gallery,
London.
Portraits of Shakespeare and many of his contemporaries.

Poets' Corner, Westminster Abbey,
London.

Royal Shakespeare Theatre, Swan Theatre and The Other Place,
Stratford-upon-Avon, Warwickshire.
For performances of plays by Shakespeare and other playwrights.

Shakespeare's Birthplace,
The Shakespeare Centre,
Stratford-upon-Avon, Warwickshire.
Shakespeare's birthplace and an exhibition of his life and background.

■ INDEX ■